Prisoners of Co

Amelia E. Barr

Alpha Editions

This edition published in 2024

ISBN 9789362512734

Design and Setting By
Alpha Editions
www.alphaedis.com
Email - info@alphaedis.com

As per information held with us this book is in Public Domain.
This book is a reproduction of an important historical work.
Alpha Editions uses the best technology to reproduce historical work
in the same manner it was first published to preserve its original nature.
Any marks or number seen are left intentionally to preserve.

Contents

I THE WEAVING OF DOOM	- 1 -
II JEALOUSY CRUEL AS THE GRAVE	- 13 -
III A SENTENCE FOR LIFE	- 26 -
IV THE DOOR WIDE OPEN	- 36 -
Book Second	- 48 -
V A NEW LIFE	- 49 -
VI KINDRED–THE QUICK AND THE DEAD	- 62 -
VII SO FAR AND NO FARTHER	- 75 -
VIII THE JUSTIFICATION OF DEATH	- 84 -
IX A SACRIFICE ACCEPTED	- 99 -
X IN THE FOURTH WATCH	- 114 -
XI THE LOWEST HELL	- 125 -
XII "AT LAST IT IS PEACE"	- 131 -

I
THE WEAVING OF DOOM

In the early part of this century there lived at Lerwick, in the Shetland Islands, a man called Liot Borson. He was no ignoble man; through sea-fishers and sea-fighters he counted his forefathers in an unbroken line back to the great Norwegian Bor, while his own life was full of perilous labor and he was off to sea every day that a boat could swim. Liot was the outcome of the most vivid and masterful form of paganism and the most vital and uncompromising form of Christianity. For nearly eight hundred years the Borsons had been christened, but who can deliver a man from his ancestors? Bor still spoke to his son through the stirring stories of the sagas, and Liot knew the lives of Thord and Odd, of Gisli and the banded men, and the tremendous drama of Nial and his sons, just as well as he knew the histories of the prophets and heroes of his Old Testament. It is true 4 that he held the former with a kind of reservation, and that he gave to the latter a devout and passionate faith, but this faith was not always potential. There were hours in Liot's life when he was still a pagan, when he approved the swift, personal vengeance which Odin enjoined and Christ forbade—hours in which he felt himself to be the son of the man who had carried his gods and his home to uninhabited Iceland rather than take cross-marking for the meek and lowly Jesus.

In his youth—before his great sorrow came to him—he had but little trouble from this subcharacter. Of all the men in Lerwick, he knew best the king stories and the tellings-up of the ancients; and when the boats with bare spars rocked idly on the summer seas waiting for the shoal, or the men and women were gathered together to pass the long winter nights, Liot was eagerly sought after. Then, as the women knit and the men sat with their hands clasped upon their heads, Liot stood in their midst and told of the wayfarings and doings of the Borsons, who had been in the Varangian Guard, and sometimes of the sad doom of his fore-elder Gisli, who had been cursed even before he was born.

He did not often speak of Gisli; for the man ruled him across the gulf of centuries, and he was always unhappy when he gave way to the temptation to do so; for he could not get rid of the sense of kinship with him, nor of the memory of that withering spaedom with which the first Gisli had been cursed by the wronged thrall who slew him—"*This is but the beginning of the ill luck which I will bring on thy kith and kin after thee.*"

Never had he felt the brooding gloom of this wretched heirship so vividly as on the night when he first met Karen Sabiston. Karen lived with her aunt Matilda Sabiston, the richest woman in Lerwick and the chief pillar of the kirk and its societies. On that night the best knitters in Lerwick were gathered at her house, knitting the fine, lace-like shawls which were to be sold at the next foy for some good cause which the minister should approve. They were weary of their own talk, and longing for Liot to come and tell them a story. And some of the young girls whispered to Karen, "When Liot Borson opens the door, then you will see the handsomest man in the islands."

"I have seen fine men in Yell and Unst," answered Karen; "I think I shall see no handsomer ones in Lerwick. Is he fair or dark?"

"He is a straight-faced, bright-faced man, tall and strong, who can tell a story so that you will be carried off your feet and away wherever he chooses to take you."

"I have done always as Karen Sabiston was minded to do; and now I will not be moved this way or that way as some one else minds."

"As to that we shall see." And as Thora Glumm spoke Liot came into the room.

"The wind is blowing dead on shore, and the sea is like a man gone out of his wits," he said.

And Matilda answered, "Well, then, Liot, come to the fire." And as they went toward the fire she stopped before a lovely girl and said, "Look, now, this is my niece Karen; she has just come from Yell, and she can tell a story also; so it will be, which can better the other."

Then Liot looked at Karen, and the girl looked up at him; in that instant their souls remembered each other. They put their hands together like old lovers, and if Liot had drawn her to his heart and kissed her Karen would not have been much astonished. This sweet reciprocity was, however, so personal that onlookers did not see it, and so swift that Liot appeared to answer promptly enough:

"It would be a good thing for us all if we should hear a new story. As for me, the game is up. I can think of nothing to-night but my poor kinsman Gisli, and he was not a lucky man, nor is it lucky to speak of him."

"Is it Gisli you are talking about?" asked Wolf Skegg. "Let us bring the man among us; I like him best of all."

"He had much sorrow," said Andrew Grimm.

"He had a good wife," answered Gust Havard; "and not many men are so lucky."

"'Twas his fate," stammered a very old man, crouching over the fire, "and in everything fate rules."

"Well, then, Snorro, fate is justice," said Matilda; "and as well begin, Liot, for it will be the tale of Gisli and no other—I see that."

Then Liot stood up, and Karen, busy with her knitting, watched him. She saw that he had brown hair and gray eyes and the fearless carriage of one who is at home on the North Sea. His voice at first was frank and full of brave inflections, as he told of the noble, faithful, helpful Gisli, pursued by evil fortune even in his dreams. Gradually its tones became sad as the complaining of the sea, and a brooding melancholy touched every heart as Gisli, doing all he might do to ward off misfortune, found it of no avail. "For what must be must be; there is no help for it," sighed Liot. "So, then, love of wife and friends, and all that good-will dared, could not help Gisli, for the man was doomed even before his birth."

Then he paused, and there was a dead silence and an unmistakable sense of expectation; and Liot's face changed, and he looked as Gisli might have looked when he knew that he had come to his last fight for life. Also for a moment his eyes rested on old Snorro, who was no longer crouching over the hearth, but straight up and full of fire and interest; and Snorro answered the look with a nod, that meant something which all approved and understood; after which Liot continued in a voice full of a somber passion:

"It was the very last night of the summer, and neither Gisli nor his true wife, Auda, could sleep. Gisli had bad dreams full of fate if he shut his eyes, and he knew that his life-days were nearly over. So they left their house and went to a hiding-place among the crags, and no sooner were they there than they heard the voice of their enemy Eyjolf, and there were fourteen men with him. 'Come on like men,' shouted Gisli, 'for I am not going to fare farther away.'"

Then old Snorro raised himself and answered Liot in the very words of Eyjolf:

"'Lay down the good arms thou bearest, and give up also Auda, thy wife.'"

"'Come and take them like a man, for neither the arms I bear nor the wife I love are fit for any one else!'" cried Liot, in reply. And this challenge and 8 valiant answer, though fully expected, charged the crowded room with enthusiasm. The women let their knitting fall and sat with parted lips and shining eyes, and the men looked at Liot as men look whose hands are on their weapons.

"So," continued Liot, "the men made for the crags; but Gisli fought like a hero, and in that bout four men were slain. And when they were least aware Gisli leaped on a crag, that stands alone there and is called Oneman's Crag, and there he turned at bay and called out to Eyjolf, 'I wish to make those three hundred in silver, which thou hast taken as the price of my head, as dear bought as I can; and before we part thou wouldst give other three hundred in silver that we had never met; for thou wilt only take disgrace for loss of life.' Then their onslaught was harder and hotter, and they gave Gisli many spear-thrusts; but he fought on wondrously, and there was not one of them without a wound who came nigh him. At last, full of great hurts, Gisli bade them wait awhile and they should have the end they wanted; for he would have time to sing this last song to his faithful Auda:

'Wife, so fair, so never-failing,

  So truly loved, so sorely cross'd,

Thou wilt often miss me, wailing;

  Thou wilt weep thy hero lost.

But my heart is stout as ever;

  Swords may bite, I feel no smart;

Father! better heirloom never

  Owned thy son than fearless heart.'

And with these words he rushed down from the crag and clove Thord—who was Eyjolf's kinsman—to the very belt. There Gisli lost his life with many great and sore wounds. He never turned his heel, and none of them saw that his strokes were lighter, the last than the first. They buried him by the sea, and at his grave the sixth man breathed his last; and on the same night the seventh man breathed his last; and an eighth lay bedridden for twelve months and died. And though the rest were healed, they got nothing but shame for their pains. Thus Gisli came to his grave; and it has always been said, by one and all, that there never was a more famous defense made by one man in any time, of which the truth is known; but he was not lucky in anything."

"I will doubt that," said Gust Havard. "He had Auda to wife, and never was there a woman more beautiful and loving and faithful. He had love-luck, if he had no other luck. God give us all such wives as Auda!"

"Well, then," answered Matilda, "a man's fate is his wife, and she is of his own choosing; and, what is more, a good husband makes a good wife." Then, suddenly stopping, she listened a moment and added: "The minister is come, and we shall hear from him still better words. But sit down, Liot; you have passed the hour well, as you always do."

The minister came in with a smile, and he was placed in the best chair and made many times welcome. It was evident in a moment that he had brought a different spirit with him; the old world vanished away, and the men and women that a few minutes before had been so close to it suffered a transformation. As the minister entered the room they became in a moment members of the straitest Christian kirk—quiet, hard-working fishers, and douce, home-keeping women. He said the night was bad and black, and spoke of the boats and the fishers in them. And the men talked solemnly about the "takes" and the kirk meetings, while some of the women knitted and listened, and others helped Matilda and Karen to set the table with goose and fish, and barley and oaten cakes, and the hot, sweet tea which is the Shetlander's favorite drink.

Many meals in a lifetime people eat, and few are remembered; but when they are "eventful," how sweet or bitter is that bread-breaking! This night Liot's cake and fish and cup of tea were as angels' food. Karen broke her cake with him, and she sweetened his cup, and smiled at him and talked to him as he ate and drank with her. And when at last they stood up for the song and thanksgiving he held her hand in his, and their voices blended in the noble sea psalm, so dear to every seafarer's heart:

"The floods, O Lord, have lifted up,

They lifted up their voice!

The floods have lifted up their waves

And made a mighty noise.

"But yet the Lord, that is on high,

Is more of might by far

Than noise of many waters is,

Or great sea-billows are."

Soft and loud the singing swelled, and the short thanksgiving followed it. To bend his head and hold Karen's hand while the blessing fell on his ears was heaven on earth to Liot; such happiness he had never known before— never even dreamed of. He walked home through the buffeting wind and the drenching rain, and felt neither; for he was saying over and over to himself, "I have found my wife! I have found my wife!"

Karen had the same prepossession. As she unbound her long, fair hair she thought of Liot. Slowly unplaiting strand from strand, she murmured to her heart as she did so:

"Such a man as Liot Borson I have never met before. It was easy to see that he loved me as soon as he looked at me; well, then, Liot Borson shall be my husband–Liot, and only Liot, will I marry."

It was at the beginning of winter that this took place, and it was a kind of new birth to Liot. Hitherto he had been a silent man about his work; he now began to talk and to sing, and even to whistle; and, as every one knows, whistling is the most cheerful sound that comes from human lips. People wondered a little and said, "It is Karen Sabiston, and it is a good thing." Also, the doubts and fears that usually trouble the beginnings of love were absent in this case. Wherever Liot and Karen had learned each other, the lesson had been perfected. At their third meeting he asked her to be his wife, and she answered with simple honesty, "That is my desire."

This betrothal was, however, far from satisfactory to Karen's aunt; she could bring up nothing against Liot, but she was ill pleased with Karen. "You have some beauty," she said, "and you have one hundred pounds of your own; and it was to be expected that you would look to better yourself a little."

"Have I not done so? Liot is the best of men."

"And the best of men are but men at best. It is not of Liot I think, but of Liot's money; he is but poor, and you know little of him. Those before us have said wisely, 'Ere you run in double harness, look well to the other horse.'"

"My heart tells me that I have done right, aunt."

"Your heart cannot foretell, but you might have sense enough to forethink; and it is sure that I little dreamed of this when I brought you here from the naked gloom of Yell."

"It is true your word brought me here, but I think it was Liot who called me by you."

"It was not. When my tongue speaks for any Borson, I wish that it may speak no more! I like none of them. Liot is good at need on a winter's night; but even so, all his stories are of dool and wrong-doing and bloody vengeance. From his own words it is seen that the Borsons have ever been well-hated men. Now, I have forty years more of this life than you have, and I tell you plainly I think little of your choice; whatever sorrow comes of it, mind this: I didn't give you leave to make it."

"Nor did I ask your leave, aunt; each heart knows its own; but you have a way to throw cold water upon every hope."

"There are hopes I wish at the bottom of the sea. To be sure, when ill is fated some one must speak the words that bring it about; but I wish it had been any other but myself who wrote, 'Come to Lerwick'; for I little thought I was writing, 'Come to Liot Borson.' As every one knows, he is the son of unlucky folk; from father to son nothing goes well with them."

"I will put my luck to his, and you will learn to think better of Liot for my sake, aunt."

"Not while my life-days last! That is a naked say, and there's no more to it."

Matilda's dislike, however, did not seriously interfere with Liot's and Karen's happiness. It was more passive than active; it was more virulent when he was absent than when he was present; and all winter she suffered him to visit at her house. These visits had various fortunes, but, good or bad, the season wore away with them; and as soon as April came Liot began to build his house. Matilda scoffed at his hurry. "Does he think," she cried, "that he can marry Karen Sabiston when he lists to? Till you are twenty-one you are in my charge, and I will take care to prevent such folly as long as I can."

"Well, then, aunt, I shall be of age and my own mistress next Christmas, and on Uphellya night[1] I will be married to Liot."

"After that we shall have nothing to say to each other."

"It will not be my fault."

"It will be my will. However, if you are in love with ill luck and fated for Liot Borson, you must dree your destiny; and Liot does well to build his home, for he shall not wive himself out of my walls."

"It will be more shame to you than to me, aunt, if I am not married from your house; also, people will speak evil of you."

"That is to be expected; but I will not be so ill to myself as to make a feast for a man I hate. However, there are eight months before Uphellya, and many chances and changes may come in eight months."

The words were a prophecy. As Matilda uttered them Thora Fay entered the room, all aglow with excitement. "There is a new ship in the harbor!" she cried. "She is called the *Frigate Bird*, and she has silk and linen and gold ornaments for sale, besides tea and coffee and the finest of spirits. As for the captain, he is as handsome as can be, and my brother thinks him a man of some account."

"You bring good news, Thora," said Matilda. "I would gladly see the best of whatever is for sale, and I wish your brother to let so much come to the man's ears."

"I will look to that," answered Thora. "Every one knows there is to be a wedding in your house very soon." And with these words she nodded at Karen, and went smiling away with her message.

A few hours afterward Captain Bele Trenby of the *Frigate Bird* stepped across Matilda Sabiston's threshold. It was the first step toward his death-place, though he knew it not; he took it with a laugh and a saucy compliment to the pretty servant who opened the door for him, and with the air of one accustomed to being welcome went into Matilda Sabiston's presence. He delighted the proud, wilful old woman as soon as she saw him; his black eyes and curling black hair, the dare-devil look on his face, and the fearless dash of his manner reminded her of Paul Sabiston, the husband of her youth. She opened her heart and her purse to the bold free-trader; she made him eat and drink, and with a singular imprudence told him of secret ways in and out of the voes, and of hiding-places in the coast caverns that had been known to her husband. And as she talked she grew handsome; so much so that Karen let her knitting fall to watch her aunt's face as she described Paul Sabiston's swift cutter—"a mass of snowy canvas, stealing in and out of the harbor like a cloud."

The coming of this man was the beginning of sorrow. In a few days he understood the situation, and he resolved to marry Karen Sabiston. Her fair, stately beauty charmed him, and he had no doubt she would inherit her aunt's wealth; that she was cold and shy only stimulated his love, and as for Liot, he held his pretensions in contempt. All summer he sailed between Holland and Shetland, and the Lerwick people gave him good trade and good welcome. With Matilda Sabiston he had his own way; she did whatever he wished her to do. Only at Karen her power stopped short; neither promises nor threats would induce the girl to accept Bele as her lover; and Matilda, accustomed to drive her will through the teeth of every one, was angry morning, noon, and night with her disobedient niece.

As the months wore on Liot's position became more and more painful and humiliating, and he had hard work to keep his hands off Bele when they met on the pier or in the narrow streets of the town. His smile, his voice, his face, his showy dress and hectoring manner, all fed in Liot's heart that bitter hatred which springs from a sense of being personally held in contempt; he felt, also, that even among his fellow-townsmen he was belittled and injured by this plausible, handsome stranger. For Bele said very much what it pleased him to say, covering his insolences with a laugh and with a jovial, jocular air, that made resentment seem ridiculous. Bele was also a gift-giver, and for every woman, old or young, he had a compliment or a ribbon.

If Liot had been less human, if he had come from a more mixed race, if his feelings had been educated down and toned to the level of modern culture, he could possibly have looked forward to Uphellya night, and found in the joy and triumph that Karen would then give him a sufficient set-off to all Bele's injuries and impertinences. But he was not made thus; his very blood came to him through the hearts of vikings and berserkers, and as long as one drop of this fierce stream remained in his veins, moments were sure to come in the which it would render all the tide of life insurgent.

It is true Liot was a Christian and a good man; but it must be noted, in order to do him full justice, that the form of Christianity which was finally and passionately accepted by his race was that of ultra-Calvinism; it spoke to their inherited tendencies as no other creed could have done. This uncompromising theology, with its God of vengeance and inflexible justice, was understood by men who considered a blood-feud of centuries a duty never to be neglected; and as for the doctrine of a special election, with all its tremendous possibilities of damnation, they were not disposed to object to it. Indeed, they were such good haters that Tophet and everlasting enmity were the bane and doom they would have unhesitatingly chosen for their enemies. This grim theology Liot sucked in with his mother's milk, and both by inheritance and by a strong personal faith he was a child of God after the order of John Calvin.

Therefore he constantly brought his enemy to the ultimate and immutable tribunal of his faith, and just as constantly condemned him there. Nothing was surer in Liot's mind than that Bele Trenby was the child of the Evil One and an inheritor of the kingdom of wrath; for Bele did the works of his father every day, and every hour of the day, and Liot told himself that it was impossible there should be any fellowship between them. To Bele he said nothing of this spiritual superiority, and yet it was obvious in his constant air of disapproval and dissent, in his lofty silence, his way of not being conscious of Bele's presence or of totally ignoring his remarks.

"Liot Borson mocks the very heart of me," said Bele to Matilda one day, as he gloomily flung himself into the big chair she pushed toward him.

"What said he, Bele?"

"Not a word with his tongue, or I had struck him in the face; but as I was telling about my last cargo and the run for it, his eyes called me '*Liar! liar! liar!*' like blow on blow. And when he turned and walked off the pier some were quiet, and some followed him; and I could have slain every man's son of them, one on the heels of the other."

"That is vain babble, Bele; and I would leave Liot alone. He has more shapes than one, and he is ill to anger in any of them."

Bele was not averse to be so counseled. In spite of his bravado and risky ventures, he was no more a brave man than a dishonorable or dishonest man ever is. He knew that if it came to fighting he would be like a child in Liot's big hands, and he had already seen Liot's scornful silence strip his boasting naked. So he contented himself with the revenge of the coward— the shrug and the innuendo, the straight up-and-down lie, when Liot was absent; the sulky nod or bantering remark, according to his humor, when Liot was present.

However, as the weeks went on Liot became accustomed to the struggle, and more able to take possession of such aids to mastery of himself as were his own. First, there was Karen; her loyalty never wavered. If Liot knew anything surely, it was that at Christmas she would become his wife. She met him whenever she could, she sent him constantly tokens of her love, and she begged him at every opportunity for her sake to let Bele Trenby alone. Every day, also, his cousin Paul Borson spoke to him and praised him for his forbearance; and every Sabbath the minister asked, "How goes it, Liot? Is His grace yet sufficient?" And at these questions Liot's countenance would glow as he answered gladly, "So far He has helped me."

From this catechism, and the clasp and look that gave it living sympathy, Liot always turned homeward full of such strength that he longed to meet his enemy on the road, just that he might show him that "noble not caring," which was gall and wormwood to Bele's touchy self-conceit. It was a great spiritual weakness, and one which Liot was not likely to combat; for prayer was so vital a thing to him that it became imbued with all his personal characteristics. He made petition that God would keep him from hurting Bele Trenby, and yet in his heart he was afraid that God would hear and grant his prayer. The pagan in Liot was not dead; and the same fight between the old man and the new man that made Paul's life a constant warfare found a fresh battle-ground in Liot's soul.

He began his devotions in the spirit of Christ, but they ended always in a passionate arraignment of Bele Trenby through the psalms of David. These wondrously human measures got Liot's heart in their grip; he wept them and prayed them and lived them until their words blended with all his thoughts and speech; through them he grew "familiar" with God, as Job and David and Jonah were familiar—a reverent familiarity. Liot ventured to tell Him all that he had to suffer from Bele—the lies that he could not refute, the insolences he could not return, his restricted intercourse with Karen, and the loss of that frank fellowship with such of his townsmen as had business reasons for not quarreling with Bele.

So matters went on, and the feeling grew no better, but worse, between the men. When the devil could not find a man to irritate Bele and Liot, then he found Matilda Sabiston always ready to speak for him. She twitted Bele with his prudences, and if she met Liot on the street she complimented him on his patience, and prophesied for Karen a "lowly mannered husband, whom she could put under her feet."

One day in October affairs all round were at their utmost strain. The summer was over, and Bele was not likely to make the Shetland coast often till after March. His talk was of the French and Dutch ports and their many attractions. And Matilda was cross at the prospect of losing her favorite's society, and unjustly inclined to blame Bele for his want of success with her niece.

"Talk if you want to, Bele," she said snappishly, "of the pretty women in France and Holland. You are, after all, a great dreamer, and you don't dream true; the fisherman Liot can win where you lose."

Then Bele said some words about Liot, and Matilda laughed. Bele thought the laugh full of scorn; so he got up and left the house in a passion, and Matilda immediately turned on Karen.

"Ill luck came with you, girl," she cried, "and I wish that Christmas was here and that you were out of my house."

"No need to wait till Christmas, aunt; I will go away now and never come back."

"I shall be glad of that."

"Paul Borson will give me shelter until I move into my own house."

"Then we shall be far apart. I shall not be sorry, for our chimneys may smoke the better for it."

"That is an unkind thing to say."

"It is as you take it."

"I wonder what people will think of you, aunt?"

"I wonder that, too–but I care nothing."

"I see that talk will come to little, and that we had better part."

"If you will marry Bele we need not part; then I will be good to you."

"I will not marry Bele–no, not for the round world."

"Then, what I have to say is this, and I say it out: go to the Borsons as soon as you can; there is doubtless soul-kin between you and them, and I want no Borson near me, in the body or out of the body."

So that afternoon Karen went to live with Paul Borson, and there was great talk about it. No sooner had Liot put his foot ashore than he heard the story, and at once he set it bitterly down against Bele; for his sake Karen had been driven from her home. There were those that said it was Bele's plan, since she would not marry him, to separate her from her aunt; he was at least determined not to lose what money and property Matilda Sabiston had to leave. These accusations were not without effect. Liot believed his rival capable of any meanness. But it was not the question of money that at this hour angered him; it was Karen's tears; it was Karen's sense of shame in being sent from the home of her only relative, and the certain knowledge that the story would be in every one's mouth. These things roused in Liot's soul hatred implacable and unmerciful and thirsty for the stream of life.

Yet he kept himself well in hand, saying little to Karen but those things usually whispered to beloved women who are weeping, and at the end of them this entreaty:

"Listen, dear heart of mine! I will see the minister, and he will call our names in the kirk next Sunday, and the next day we shall be married, and then there will be an end to this trouble. I say nothing of Matilda Sabiston, but Bele Trenby stirs up bickerings all day long; he is a low, quarrelsome fellow, a very son of Satan, walking about the world tempting good men to sin."

And Karen answered: "Life is full of waesomeness. I have always heard that when the heart learns to love it learns to sorrow; yet for all this, and more too, I will be your wife, Liot, on the day you wish, for then if sorrow comes we two together can well bear it."

---

[1]
The last day of Christmas-tide.

<hr size=2 width="100%" align=center>

II
JEALOUSY CRUEL AS THE GRAVE

After this event all Lerwick knew that Karen Sabiston was to be married to Liot Borson in less than three weeks. For the minister was unwilling to shorten the usual time for the kirk calling, and Karen, on reflection, had also come to the conclusion that it was best not to hurry too much. "Everything ought to bide its time, Liot," she said, "and the minister wishes the three askings to be honored; also, as the days go by, my aunt may think better and do better than she is now minded to."

"If I had my way, Karen—"

"But just now, Liot, it is my way."

"Yours and the minister's."

"Then it is like to be good."

"Well, let it stand at three weeks; but I wish that the time had not been put off; ill luck comes to a changed wedding-day."

"Why do you forespeak misfortune, Liot? It is a bad thing to do. Far better if you went to the house-builder and told him to hire more help and get the roof-tree on; then we need not ask shelter either from kin or kind."

It was a prudent thought, and Liot acknowledged its wisdom and said he would "there and then go about it." The day was nearly spent, but the moon was at its full, and the way across the moor was as well known to him as the space of his own boat. He kissed Karen fondly, and promised to return in two or three hours at the most; and she watched his tall form swing into the shadows and become part and parcel of the gray indistinctness which shut in the horizon.

There was really no road to the little hamlet where the builder lived. The people used the sea road, and thought it good enough; but the rising moon showed a foot-path, like a pale, narrow ribbon, winding through the peat-cuttings and skirting the still, black moss waters. But in this locality Liot had cut many a load of peat, and he knew the bottomless streams of the heath as well as he knew the "races" of the coast; so he strode rapidly forward on his pleasant errand.

The builder, who was also a fisherman, had just come from the sea; and as he ate his evening meal he talked with Liot about the new house, and promised him to get help enough to finish it within a month. This business occupied about an hour, and as soon as it was over Liot lit his pipe and took the way homeward. He had scarcely left the sea-shore when he saw a man before him, walking very slowly and irresolutely; and Liot said to himself, "He steps like one who is not sure of his way." With the thought he called out, "*Take care!*" and hastened forward; and the man stood still and waited for him.

In a few minutes Liot also wished to stand still; for the moon came from behind a cloud and showed him plainly that the wayfarer was Bele Trenby. The recognition was mutual, but for once Bele was disposed to be conciliating. He was afraid to turn back and equally afraid to go forward; twice already the moonlight had deceived him, and he had nearly stepped into the water; so he thought it worth his while to say:

"Good evening, Liot; I am glad you came this road; it is a bad one–a devilish bad one! I wish I had taken a boat. I shall miss the tide, and I was looking to sail with it. It is an hour since I passed Skegg's Point–a full hour, for it has been a step at a time. Now you will let me step after you; I see you know the way."

He spoke with a nervous rapidity, and Liot only answered:

"Step as you wish to."

Bele fell a couple of feet behind, but continued to talk. "I have been round Skegg's Point," he said with a chuckling laugh. "I wanted to see Auda Brent before I went away for the winter. Lovely woman! Brent is a lucky fellow–"

"Brent is my friend," answered Liot, angrily. But Bele did not notice the tone, and he continued:

"I would rather have Auda for a friend." And then, in his usual insinuating, boastful way, he praised the woman's beauty and graciousness in words which had an indefinable offense, and yet one quite capable of that laughing denial which commonly shielded Bele's impertinence. "Brent gave me a piece of Saxony cloth and a gold brooch for her–Brent is in Amsterdam. I have taken the cloth four times; there were also other gifts–but I will say nothing of them."

"You are inventing lies, Bele Trenby. Touch your tongue, and your fingers will come out of your lips black as the pit. Say to Brent what you have said to me. You dare not, you infernal coward!"

"You have a pretty list of bad words, Liot, and I won't try to change mine with them."

Liot did not answer. He turned and looked at the man behind him, and the devil entered into his heart and whispered, "*There is the venn before you.*" The words were audible to him; they set his heart on fire and made his blood rush into his face, and beat on his ear-drums like thunder. He could scarcely stand. A fierce joy ran through his veins, and the fiery radiations of his life colored the air around him; he saw everything red. The venn, a narrow morass with only one safe crossing, was before them; in a few moments they were on its margin. Liot suddenly stopped; the leather strings of his *rivlins*[2] had come unfastened, and he dropped the stick he carried in order to retie them. At this point there was a slight elevation on the morass, and Bele looked at Liot as he put his foot upon it, asking sharply:

"Is this the crossing?"

Liot fumbled at his shoe-strings and said not a word; for he knew it was *not* the crossing.

"Is this the crossing, Liot?" Bele again asked. And again Liot answered neither yes nor no. Then Bele flew into a passion and cried out with an oath:

"You are a cursed fellow, Liot Borson, and in the devil's own temper; I will stay no longer with you."

He stepped forward as he spoke, and instantly a cry, shrill with mortal terror, rang across the moor from sea to sea. Liot quickly raised himself, but he had barely time to distinguish the white horror of his enemy's face and the despair of his upthrown arms. The next moment the moss had swallowed the man, and the thick, peaty water hardly stirred over his engulfing.

For a little while Liot fixed his eyes on the spot; then he lifted his stick and went forward, telling his soul in triumphant undertones: "He has gone down quick into hell; the Lord has brought him down into the pit of destruction; the bloody and deceitful man shall not live out half his days; he has gone to his own place."

Over and over he reiterated these assurances, stepping securely himself to the ring of their doom. It was not until he saw the light in Paul Borson's house that the chill of doubt and the sickness of fear assailed him. How could he smile into Karen's face or clasp her to his breast again? A candle was glimmering in the window of a fisherman's cottage; he stepped into its light and looked at his hands. There was no stain of blood on them, but he was angry at the involuntary act; he felt it to be an accusation.

Just yet he could not meet Karen. He walked to the pier, and talked to his conscience as he did so. "I never touched the man," he urged. "I said nothing to lead him wrong. He was full of evil; his last words were such as slay a woman's honor. I did right not to answer him. A hundred times I have vowed I would not turn a finger to save his life, and God heard and knew my vow. He delivered him into my hand; he let me see the end of the wicked. I am not to blame! I am not to blame!" Then said an interior voice, that he had not silenced, "Go and tell the sheriff what has happened."

Liot turned home at this advice. Why should he speak now? Bele was dead and buried; let his memory perish with him. He summoned from every nook of his being all the strength of the past, the present, and the future, and with a resolute hand lifted the latch of the door. Karen threw down her knitting and ran to meet him; and when he had kissed her once he felt that the worst was over. Paul asked him about the house, and talked over his plans and probabilities, and after an interval he said:

"I saw Bele Trenby's ship was ready for sea at the noon hour; she will be miles away by this time. It is a good thing, for Mistress Sabiston may now come to reason."

"It will make no odds to us; we shall not be the better for Bele's absence."

"I think differently. He is one of the worst of men, and he makes everything grow in Matilda's eyes as he wishes to. Lerwick can well spare him; a bad man, as every one knows."

"A man that joys the devil. Let us not speak of him."

"But he speaks of you."

"His words will not slay me. Kinsman, let us go to sleep now; I am promised to the fishing with the early tide."

But Liot could not sleep. In vain he closed his eyes; they saw more than he could tell. There were invisible feet in his room; the air was heavy with presence, and full of vague, miserable visions; for "Wickedness, condemned by her own witness, is very timorous, and, being pressed with Conscience, always forecasteth grievous things."

When Bele stepped into his grave there had been a bright moonlight blending with the green, opalish light of the aurora charging to the zenith; and in this mysterious mingled glow Liot had seen for a moment the white, upturned face that the next moment went down with open eyes into the bottomless water. Now, though the night had become dark and stormy, he could not dismiss the sight, and anon the Awful One who dwelleth in the thick darkness drew near, and for the first time in his life Liot Borson was afraid. Then it was that his deep and real religious life came to his help. He rose, and stood with clasped hands in the middle of the room, and began to plead his cause, even as Job did in the night of his terror. In his strong, simple speech he told everything to God—told him the wrongs that had been done him, the provocations he had endured. His solemnly low implorations were drenched with agonizing tears, and they only ceased when the dayspring came and drove the somber terrors of the night before it.

Then he took his boat and went off to sea, though the waves were black and the wind whistling loud and shrill. He wanted the loneliness that only the sea could give him. He felt that he must "cry aloud" for deliverance from the great strait into which he had fallen. No man could help him, no human sympathy come between him and his God. Into such communions not even the angels enter.

At sundown he came home, his boat loaded with fish, and his soul quiet as the sea was quiet after the storm had spent itself. Karen said he "looked as if he had seen Death"; and Paul answered: "No wonder at that; a man in an open boat in such weather came near to him." Others spoke of his pallor and his weariness; but no one saw on his face that mystical self-signature of submission which comes only through the pang of soul-travail.

He had scarcely changed his clothing and sat down to his tea before Paul said: "A strange thing has happened. Trenby's ship is still in harbor. He cannot be found; no one has seen him since he left the ship yesterday. He bade Matilda Sabiston good-by in the morning, and in the afternoon he told his men to be ready to lift anchor when the tide turned. The tide turned, but he came not; and they wondered at it, but were not anxious; now, however, there is a great fear about him."

"What fear is there?" asked Liot.

"Men know not; but it is uppermost in all minds that in some way his life-days are ended."

"Well, then, long or short, it is God who numbers our days."

"What do you think of the matter?" asked Paul.

"As you know, kinsman," answered Liot, "I have ever hated Bele, and that with reason. Often I have said it were well if he were hurt, and better if he were dead; but at this time I will say no word, good or bad. If the man lives, I have nothing good to say of him; if he is dead, I have nothing bad to say."

"That is wise. Our fathers believed in and feared the fetches of dead men; they thought them to be not far away from the living, and able to be either good friends or bitter enemies to them."

"I have heard that often. No saying is older than 'Bare is a man's back without the kin behind him.'"

"Then you are well clad, Liot, for behind you are generations of brave and good men."

"The Lord is at my right hand; I shall not be moved," said Liot, solemnly. "He is sufficient. I am as one of the covenanted, for the promise is 'to you and your children.'"

Paul nodded gravely. He was a Calvinistic pagan, learned in the Scriptures, inflexible in faith, yet by no means forgetful of the potent influences of his heroic dead. Truly he trusted in the Lord, but he was never unwilling to remember that Bor and Bor's mighty sons stood at his back. Even though they were in the "valley of shadows," they were near enough in a strait to divine his trouble and be ready to help him.

The tenor of this conversation suited both men. They pursued it in a fitful manner and with long, thoughtful pauses until the night was far spent; then they said, "Good sleep," with a look into each other's eyes which held not only promise of present good-will, but a positive "looking forward" neither cared to speak more definitely of.

The next day there was an organized search for Bele Trenby through the island hamlets and along the coast; but the man was not found far or near; he had disappeared as absolutely as a stone dropped into mid-ocean. Not until the fourth day was there any probable clue found; then a fishing-smack came in, bringing a little rowboat usually tied to Howard Hallgrim's rock. Hallgrim was a very old man and had not been out of his house for a week, so that it was only when the boat was found at sea that it was missed from its place. It was then plain to every one that Bele had taken the boat for some visit and met with an accident.

So far the inference was correct. Bele's own boat being shipped ready for the voyage, he took Hallgrim's boat when he went to see Auda Brent; but he either tied it carelessly or he did not know the power of the tide at that point, for when he wished to return the boat was not there. For a few minutes he hesitated; he was well aware that the foot-path across the moor was a dangerous one, but he was anxious to leave Lerwick with that tide, and he risked it.

These facts flashed across Liot's mind with the force of truth, and he never doubted them. All, then, hung upon Auda Brent's reticence; if she admitted that Bele had called on her that afternoon, some one would divine the loss of the boat and the subsequent tragedy. For several wretched days he waited to hear the words that would point suspicion to him. They were not spoken. Auda came to Lerwick, as usual, with her basket of eggs for sale; she talked with Paul Borson about Bele's disappearance; and though Liot watched her closely, he noticed neither tremor nor hesitation in her face or voice. He thought, indeed, that she showed very little feeling of any kind in the matter. It took him some time to reach the conclusion that Auda was playing a part—one she thought best for her honor and peace.

A LERWICK MAN.

In the mean time the preparations for his marriage with Karen Sabiston went rapidly forward. He strove to keep his mind and heart in tune with them, but it was often hard work. Sometimes Karen questioned him concerning his obvious depression; sometimes she herself caught the infection of his sadness; and there were little shadows upon their love that she could not understand. On the day before her marriage she went to visit her aunt Matilda Sabiston. Matilda did not deny herself, but afterward Karen wished she had done so. Almost her first words were of Bele Trenby, for whom she was mourning with the love of a mother for an only son.

"What brings you into my sight?" she asked the girl. "Bele is dead and gone, and you are living! and Liot Borson knows all about it!"

"How dare you say such a thing, aunt?"

"I can dare the truth, though the devil listened to it. As for 'aunt,' I am no aunt of yours."

"I am content to be denied by you; and I will see that Liot makes you pay dearly for the words that you have said."

"No fear! he will not dare to challenge them! I know that."

"You have called him a murderer!"

"He did the deed, or he has knowledge of it. *One* who never yet deceived me tells me so much. Oh, if I could only bring that *one* into the court I would hang Liot higher than his masthead! I wish to die only that I may follow Liot, and give him misery on misery every one of his life-days. I would also poison his sleep and make his dreams torture him. If there is yet one kinsman behind my back, I will force him to dog Liot into the grave."

"Liot is in the shelter of God's hand; he need not fear what you can do to him. He can prove you liar far easier than you can prove him murderer. On the last day of Bele's life Liot was at sea all day, and there were three men with him. He spent the evening with John Twatt and myself, and then sat until the midnight with Paul Borson."

"For all that, he was with Bele Trenby! I know it! My heart tells me so."

"Your heart has often lied to you before this. I see, however, that our talk had better come to an end once for all. I will never come here again."

"I shall be the happier for that. Why did you come at this time?"

"I thought that you were in trouble about Bele. I was sorry for you. I wished to be friends with every one before I married."

"I want no pity; I want vengeance; and from here or *there* I will compass it. While my head is above the mold there is no friendship possible between us—no, nor after it. Do you think that Bele is out of your way because he is out of the body? He is now nearer to you than your hands or feet. And let

Liot Borson look to himself. The old thrall's curse was evil enough, but Bele Trenby will make it measureless."

"Such words are like the rest of your lying; I will not fear them, since God is himself, and he shall rule the life Liot and I will lead together. When a girl is near her bridal every one but you will give her a blessing. I think you have no heart; surely you never loved any one."

"I have loved–*yes*!" Then she stood up and cried passionately: "Begone! I will speak no more to you–only this: ask Liot Borson what was the ending of Bele Trenby."

She was the incarnation of rage and accusation, and Karen almost fled from her presence. Her first impulse was to go to Liot with the story of the interview, but her second was a positive withdrawal of it. It was the eve of her bridal day, and the house was already full of strangers. Paul Borson was spending his money freely for the wedding-feast. In the morning she was to become Liot's wife. How could she bring contention where there should be only peace and good-will?

Besides, Liot had told her it was useless to visit Matilda; he had even urged her not to do so, for all Lerwick knew how bitterly she was lamenting the loss of her adopted son Bele; and Liot had said plainly to Karen: "As for her good-will, there is more hope of the dead; let her alone." As she remembered these words a cold fear invaded Karen's heart; it turned her sick even to dismiss it. What if Liot did know the ending of Bele! She recalled with a reluctant shiver his altered behavior, his long silences, his gloomy restlessness, the frequent breath of some icy separation between them. If Matilda was right in any measure–if Liot knew! Merciful God, if Liot had had any share in the matter! She could not face him with such a thought in her heart. She ran down to the sea-shore, and hid herself in a rocky shelter, and tried to think the position down to the bottom.

It was all a chaos of miserable suspicion, and at last she concluded that her fear and doubt came entirely from Matilda's wicked assertions. She would not admit that they had found in her heart a condition ready to receive them. She said: "I will not again think of the evil words; it is a wrong to Liot. I will not tell them to him; he would go to Matilda, and there would be more trouble, and the why and the wherefore spread abroad; and God knows how the wicked thought grows."

Then she stooped and bathed her eyes and face in the cold salt water, and afterward walked slowly back to Paul Borson's. The house was full of company and merry-making, and she was forced to fall into the mood expected from her. Women do such things by supreme efforts beyond the power of men. And Karen's smiles showed nothing of the shadow behind them, even when Liot questioned her about her visit.

"She is a bad woman, Liot," answered Karen, "and she said many temper-trying words."

"That is what I looked for, Karen. It is her way about all things to scold and storm her utmost. Does she trouble you, dear one?"

"I will not be word-sick for her. There is, as you said, no love lost between us, and I shall not care a rap for her anger. Thanks to the Best, we can live without her." And in this great trust she laid her hand in Liot's, and all shadows fled away.

It was then a lovely night, bright with rosy auroras; but before morning there was a storm. The bridal march to the kirk had to be given up, and, hooded and cloaked, the company went to the ceremony as they best could. There was no note of music to step to; it was hard enough to breast the gusty, rattling showers, and the whole landscape was a little tragedy of wind and rain, of black, tossing seas and black, driving clouds. Many who were not at the bridal shook their heads at the storm-drenched wedding-guests, and predicted an unhappy marriage; and a few ventured to assert that Matilda Sabiston had been seen going to the spaewife Asta. "And what for," they asked, "but to buy charms for evil weather?"

All such dark predictions, however, appeared to be negatived by actual facts. No man in Lerwick was so happy as Liot Borson. The home he had built Karen made a marvel of neatness and even beauty; it was always spotless and tidy, and full of bits of bright color–gay patchwork and crockery, and a snow-white hearth with its glow of fiery peat. Always she was ready to welcome him home with a loving kiss and all the material comforts his toil required. *And they loved each other!* When that has been said, what remains unsaid? It covers the whole ground of earthly happiness.

How the first shadow crossed the threshold of this happy home neither Liot nor Karen could tell; it came without observation. It was in the air, and entered as subtly and as silently. Liot noticed it first. It began with the return of Brent. When he gave Bele the piece of cloth and the gold brooch for his wife, he was on the point of leaving Amsterdam for Java. Fever and various other things delayed his return, but in the end he came back to Lerwick and began to talk about Bele. For Auda, reticent until her husband's return, then told him of Bele's visit; and one speculation grew on the top of another until something like the truth was in all men's minds, even though it was not spoken. Liot saw the thought forming in eyes that looked at him; he felt it in little reluctances of his mates, and heard it, or thought he heard it, in their voices. He took home with him the unhappy hesitation or misgiving, and watched to see if it would touch the consciousness of Karen. The loving wife, just approaching the perilous happiness of maternity, kept asking herself, "What is it? What is it?" And the answer was ever the same—the accusing words that Matilda Sabiston had said, and the quick, sick terror of heart they had awakened.

On Christmas day Karen had a son, a child of extraordinary beauty, that brought his soul into the world with him. The women said that his eyes instantly followed the light, and that his birth-cry passed into a smile. Liot was solemnly and silently happy. He sat for hours holding his wife's hand and watching the little lad sleeping so sweetly after his first hard travail; for the birth of this child meant to Liot far more than any mortal comprehended. He knew himself to be of religiously royal ancestry, and the covenant of God to such ran distinctly, *"To you and your children."* So, then, if God had refused him children, he would certainly have believed that for his sin in regard to Bele Trenby the covenant between God and the Borsons was broken. This fair babe was a renewal of it. He took him in his arms with a prayer of inexpressible thanksgiving. He kissed the child, and called him David with the kiss, and said to his soul, "The Lord hath accepted my contrition."

For some weeks this still and perfect happiness continued. The days were dark and stormy, and the nights long; but in Liot's home there was the sunlight of a woman's face and the music of a baby's voice. The early spring brought the first anxiety, for it brought with it no renewal of Karen's health and strength. She had the look of a leaf that is just beginning to droop upon its stem, and Liot watched her from day to day with a sick anxiety. He made her go to sea with him, and laughed with joy when the keen winds brought back the bright color to her cheeks. But it was only a momentary flush, bought at far too great a price of vitality. In a few weeks she could not pay the price, and the heat of the summer prostrated her. She had drooped in the spring; in the autumn she faded away. When Christmas came again there was no longer any hope left in Liot's broken heart; he knew she was dying. Night and day he was at her side, there was so much to say to each other; for only God knew how long they were to be parted, or in what place of his great universe they should meet again.

At the end of February it had come to this acknowledgment between them. Sometimes Liot sat with dry eyes, listening to Karen's sweet hopes of their reunion; sometimes he laid his head upon her pillow and wept such tears as leave life ever afterward dry at its source. And the root of this bitterness was Bele Trenby. If it had not been for this man Liot could have shared his wife's hopes and said farewell to her with the thought of heaven in his heart; but the very memory of Bele sank him below the tide of hope. God was even then "entering into judgment with him," and what if he should not be able to endure unto the end, and so win, though hardly, a painful acceptance? In every phase and form such thoughts haunted the wretched man continually. And surely Karen divined it, for all her sweet efforts were to fill his heart with a loving "looking forward" to their meeting, and a confident trust in God's everlasting mercy.

One stormy night in March she woke from a deep slumber and called Liot. Her voice had that penetrating intelligence of the dying which never deceives, and Liot knew instantly that the hour for parting had come. He took her hands and murmured in tones of anguish, "O Karen, Karen! wife of my soul!"

She drew him closer, and said with the eagerness of one in great haste, "Oh, my dear one, I shall soon be nearer to God than you. At his feet I will pray. Tell me—tell me quick, what shall I ask for you? Liot, dear one, tell me!"

"Ask that I may be forgiven *all* my sins."

"Is there one great sin, dear one? Oh, tell me now—one about Bele Trenby? Speak quickly, Liot. Did you see him die?"

"I did, but I hurt him not."

"He went into the moss?"

"Yes."

"You could have saved him and did not?"

"If I had spoken in time; there was but a single moment—I know not what prevented me. O Karen, I have suffered! I have suffered a thousand deaths!"

"My dear one, I have known it. Now we will pray together—I in heaven, thou on earth. Fear not, dear, dear Liot; he spareth all; they are his. The Lord is the lover of souls."

These were her last words. With clasped hands and wide-open eyes she lay still, watching and listening, ready to follow when beckoned, and looking with fixed vision, as if seeing things invisible, into the darkness she was about to penetrate. Steeped to his lips in anguish, Liot stood motionless until a dying breath fluttered through the room; and he knew by his sudden sense of loss and loneliness that she was gone, and that for this life he was alone forevermore.

[2]

Shoes made of untanned cowhide.

<hr size=2 width="100%" align=center>

III
A SENTENCE FOR LIFE

All Lerwick had been anticipating the death of Karen, but when it came there was a shock. She was so young and so well loved, besides which her affectionate heart hid a great spirit; and there was a general hope that for her husband's and child's sake she would hold on to life. For, in spite of all reasoning, there remains deep in the heart of man a sense of mastery over his own destiny—a conviction that we do not die until we are willing to die. We "resign" our spirits; we "commit" them to our Creator; we "*give up* the ghost"; and it did not seem possible to the wives and mothers of Lerwick that Karen would "give up" living. Her mortality was so finely blended with her immortality, it was hard to believe in such early dissolution. Alas! the finer the nature, the more readily it is fretted to decay by underlying wrong or doubt. When Matilda Sabiston drove Karen down to the sea-shore on the day before her bridal she really gave her the death-blow.

For Karen needed more than the bread and love of mortal life to sustain her. She belonged to that high order of human beings who require a sure approval of conscience even for their physical health, and whose house of life, wanting this fine cement, easily falls to dissolution. Did she, then, doubt her husband? Did she believe Matilda's accusations to be true? Karen asked herself these questions very often, and always answered them with strong assurances of Liot's innocence; but nevertheless they became part of her existence. No mental decisions, nor even actual words, could drive them from the citadel they had entered. Though she never mentioned the subject to Liot, though she watched herself continually lest any such doubts should darken her smiles or chill her love, yet they insensibly impregnated the house in which they dwelt with her. Liot could not say he felt them here or there, but they were all-pervading.

Karen withered in their presence, and Liot's denser soul would eventually have become sick with the same influence. It was, therefore, no calamity that spared their love such a tragic trial, and if Liot had been a man of clearer perceptions he would have understood that it was not in anger, but in mercy to both of them, that Karen had been removed to paradise. Her last words, however, had partially opened his spiritual vision. He saw what poison had defiled the springs of her life, and he knew instinctively that Matilda Sabiston was the enemy that had done the deed.

It was, therefore, little wonder that he sent her no notice of her niece's death. And, indeed, Matilda heard of it first through the bellman calling the funeral hour through the town. The day was of the stormiest, and many remembered how steadily storm and gust had attended all the great events of Karen's short life. She had been born in the tempest which sent her father to the bottom of the sea, and she herself, in coming from Yell to Lerwick, had barely escaped shipwreck. Her bridal garments had been drenched with rain, and on the day set for her baby's christening there was one of the worst of snow-storms. Indeed, many said that it was the wetting she received on that occasion which had developed the "wasting" that killed her. The same turmoil of the elements marked her burial day. A cold northeast wind drove through the wet streets, and the dreary monotony of the outside world was unspeakable.

But Matilda Sabiston looked through her dim windows without any sense of the weather's depressing influence–the storm of anger in her heart was so much more imperative. She waited impatiently for the hour appointed for the funeral, and then threw over her head and shoulders a large hood and cloak of blue flannel. She did not realize that the wind blew them backward, that her gray hairs were dripping and disarranged, and her clothing storm-draggled and unsuitable for the occasion; her one thought was to reach Liot's house about the time when the funeral guests were all assembled. She lifted the latch and entered the crowded room like a bad fate. Every one ceased whispering and looked at her.

She stepped swiftly to the side of the coffin, which was resting on two chairs in the middle of the room. Liot leaned on the one at the head; the minister stood by the one at the foot, and he was just opening the book in his hands. He looked steadily at Matilda, and there was a warning in the look, which the angry woman totally disdained. Liot never lifted his eyes; they were fixed on Karen's dead face; but his hands held mechanically a Bible, open at its proper place. But though he did not see Matilda, he knew when she entered; he felt the horror of her approach, and when she laid her hand on his arm he shook it violently off and forced himself to look into her evilly gleaming eyes.

She laughed outright. "So the curse begins," she said, "and this is but the first of it."

"This is no hour to talk of curses, Mistress Sabiston," said the minister, sternly. "If you cannot bring pity and pardon to the dead, then fear to come into their presence."

"I have nothing to fear from the dead. It is Liot Borson who is 'followed,' not me; I did not murder Bele Trenby."

"Now, then," answered the minister, "it is time there was a stop put to this talk. Speak here, before the living and the dead, the evil words you have said in the ears of so many. What have you to say against Liot Borson?"

"Look at him!" she cried. "He dares to hold in his hands the Holy Word, and I vow those hands of his are red with the blood of the man he murdered—I mean of Bele Trenby."

Liot kept his eyes fixed on her until she ceased speaking; then he turned them on the minister and said, "Speak for me."

"Speak for thyself once and for all, Liot. Speak here before God and thy dead wife and thy mates and thy townsmen. Did thy hands slay Bele Trenby? Are they indeed red with his blood?"

"I never lifted one finger against Bele Trenby. My hands are clear and clean from all blood-guiltiness." And he dropped the Word upon Karen's breast, and held up his hands in the sight of heaven and men.

"You lie!" screamed Matilda.

"God is my judge, not you," answered Liot.

"It is the word of Liot Borson. Who believes it?" asked the minister. "Let those who do so take the hands he declares guiltless of blood." And the minister clasped Liot's hands as he spoke the words, and then stepped aside to allow others to follow him. And there was not one man or woman present who did not thus openly testify to their belief in Liot's innocence. Matilda mocked them as they did so with output tongue and scornful laughs; but no one interfered until the minister said:

"Mistress Sabiston, you must now hold your peace forever."

"I will not. I will—"

"It is your word against Liot's, and your word is not believed."

Then the angry woman fell into a great rage, and railed on every one so passionately that for a few moments she carried all before her. Some of the company stood up round the coffin, as if to defend the dead; and the minister looked at Grimm and Twatt, two big fishermen, and said, "Mistress Sabiston is beside herself; take her civilly to her home." And they drew her arms within their own, and so led her storming out into the storm.

Liot had the better of his enemy, but he felt no sense of victory. He did not even see the manner of her noisy exit, for he stood in angry despair, looking down at the calm face of his dead wife. Then the door shut out the turmoil, and the solemn voice of the minister called peace into the disquieted, woeful room. Liot was insensible to the change. His whole soul was insurgent; he was ready to accuse heaven and earth of unutterable cruelty to him. Strong as his physical nature was, at this hour it was almost impotent. His feet felt too heavy to move; he saw, and he saw not; and the words that were spoken were only a chaos of sounds.

Andrew Vedder and Hal Skager took his right arm and his left, and led him to his place in the funeral procession. It was only a small one. Those not closely connected with the Borsons went to their homes after the service; for, besides the storm, the hour was late and the night closing in. It seemed as if nature showed her antagonism to poor Karen even to the last scene of her mortal drama; for the tide flowed late, and a Shetlander can only be buried with the flowing tide. The failing light, however, was but a part of the great tragedy of Liot's soul; it seemed the proper environment.

He bared his head as he took his place, and when urged to put on his hat flung it from him. The storm beat on Karen's coffin; why not on his head also? People looked at him pitifully as he passed, and an old woman, as she came out of her cottage to cast the customary three clods of earth behind the coffin, called out as she did so, "The comforts of the Father, Son, and Holy Ghost be with you, Liot." It was Margaret Borson, and she was a century old. She tottered into the storm, and a little child handed her the turf clods, which she cast with the prayer. It came from kindred lips, and so entered Liot's ears. He lifted his eyes a moment, looked at the eldrich, shadowy woman trembling in the gray light, and bowing his head said softly, "Thank you, mother."

There was not a word spoken at the open grave. Liot stood in a breathing stupor until all was over, and then got back somehow to his desolate home. Paul Borson's wife had taken the child away with her, and other women had tidied the room and left a pot of tea on the hob and a little bread and meat on the table. He was alone at last. He slipped the wooden bolt across the door, and then sat down to think and to suffer.

But the mercy of God found him out, and he fell into a deep sleep; and in that sleep he dreamed a dream, and was a little comforted. "I have sinned," he said when he awoke; "but I am His child, and I cannot slip beyond His mercy. My life shall be atonement, and I will not fear to fall into His hands."

And, thank God, no grief lasts forever. As the days and weeks wore away Liot's sorrow for his wife grew more reasonable; then the spring came and the fishing was to attend to; and anon little David began to interest his heart and make him plan for the future. He resolved to save money and send the lad to St. Andrew's, and give him to the service of the Lord. All that he longed for David should have; all that he had failed to accomplish

David should do. He would give his own life freely if by this sacrifice he could make David's life worthy to be an offering at His altar.

The dream, though it never came true, comforted and strengthened him; it was something to live for. He was sure that, wherever in God's universe Karen now dwelt, she would be glad of such a destiny for her boy. He worked cheerfully night and day for his purpose, and the work in itself rewarded him. The little home in which he had been so happy and so miserable was sold, and the money put in the bank for "David's education." All Liot's life now turned upon this one object, and, happily, it was sufficient to restore to him that hope—that something to look forward to—which is the salt of life.

Matilda gave him no further trouble. She sent him a bill for Karen's board, and he paid it without a word; and this was the last stone she could throw; besides which, she found herself compelled by public opinion to make some atonement for her outrageous behavior, since in those days it would have been as easy to live in St. Petersburg and quarrel with the czar as to live in Shetland and not have the minister's approval. So Mistress Sabiston had a special interview with the Rev. Magnus Ridlon, and she also sent a sum of money to the kirk as a "mortification," and eventually was restored to all sacred privileges, except the great one of the holy table. This depended inexorably on her public exoneration of Liot and her cultivation of good-will toward him. She utterly refused Liot, and preferred to want the sacred bread and wine rather than eat and drink them with Liot Borson. And though Liot declared his willingness to forgive Matilda fully, in his heart he was not sorry to be spared the spiritual obligation.

So the seasons wore away, and summer and winter brought work and rest, until David was nearly six years old. By this time the women of Lerwick thought Liot should look for another wife. "There is Halla Odd," said Jean Borson; "she is a widow of thine own age and she is full-handed. It is proper for thee now to make a home for thyself and David. When a wife has been dead four years there has been mourning enough."

Impatient of such talk at first, Liot finally took it into some consideration; but it always ended in one way: he cast his eyes to that lonely croft where Karen slept, and remembered words she had once spoken:

"In a little while I shall go away, Liot, and people will say, 'She is in her grave'; *but I shall not be there.*"

That was exactly Liot's feeling—Karen was not there. She had loved God and believed in heaven, and he was sure that she had gone to heaven. And from every spot on the open sea or the streeted town or the solitary moors he had only to look up to the place where his beloved dwelt. He did, however, as Jean Borson desired: he thought about Halla Odd; he watched her ways, and speculated about her money and her house skill and the likelihood of her making a good stepmother to David.

Probably, if events had taken their usual course, he would have married Halla; but at the beginning of the summer this thing happened: a fine private yacht was brought into harbor with her sails torn to rags and her mainmast injured. Coming down from the north, she had been followed and caught by a storm, and was in considerable distress when she was found by some Lerwick fisher-smacks. Then, as Liot Borson was the best sailmaker in the town, he was hired to put the yacht's canvas in good condition; and while doing so the captain of the yacht, who was also her owner, talked often with him about the different countries he had visited. He showed him paintings of famous places and many illustrated volumes of travel, and so fired Liot's heart that his imagination, like a bird, flew off in all directions.

In a short time the damaged wayfarer, with all her new sails set, went southward, and people generally forgot her visit. But Liot was no more the same man after it. He lived between the leaves of a splendid book of voyages which had been left with him. Halla went out of his thoughts and plans, and all his desires were set to one distinct purpose—to see the world, and the whole world. David was the one obstacle. He did not wish to leave him in Shetland, for his intention was to bid farewell forever to the island. It had suddenly become a prison to him; he longed to escape from it. So, then, David must be taken away or the boy would draw him back; but the question was, where should he carry the child?

He thought instantly of his sister, who was married to a man in comfortable circumstances living at Stornoway, in the Outer Hebrides, and he resolved to take David to her. He could now afford to pay well for his board and schooling, and he was such a firm believer in the tie of blood-kinship that the possibility of the child not being kindly treated never entered his mind. And as he was thinking over the matter a man came from Stornoway to the Shetland fishing, and spoke well of his sister Lizzie and her husband. He said also that their only child was in the Greenland whaling-fleet, and that David would be a godsend of love to their solitary hearts.

This report satisfied Liot, and the rest was easily managed. Paul Borson urged him to stay until the summer fishing was over; but Liot was possessed by the sole idea of getting away, and he would listen to nothing that interfered with this determination. He owned half the boat in which he fished, and as it was just at the beginning of the season he was obliged to buy the other half at an exorbitant price. But the usually prudent man would make no delays; he paid the price asked, and then quickly prepared the boat for the voyage he contemplated.

One night after David was asleep he carried him on board of her; and Paul divined his purpose, though it was unspoken. He walked with him to the boat, and they smoked their last pipe together in the moonlight on her deck, and were both very silent. Paul had told himself that he had a great deal to say to his cousin, yet when it came to the last hour they found themselves unable to talk. At midnight both men stood up.

"The tide serves," said Liot, softly, holding out his hand.

And Paul clasped it and answered: "God be with thee, Liot."

"We shall meet no more in this life, Paul."

"Then I tryst thee for the next life; that will be a good meeting. Fare thee well. God keep thee!"

"THE WATERS OF THE GREAT DEEP."

"And thee also."

"Then we shall be well kept, both of us."

That was the last of Shetland for Liot Borson. He watched his kinsman out of sight, and then lifted his anchor, and in the silence and moonlight went out to sea. When the Lerwick people awoke in the morning Liot was miles and miles away. He was soon forgotten. It was understood that he would never come back, and there was no more interest in him than there is in the dead. Like them, he had had his time of sojourn, and his place knew him no more.

As for Liot, he was happy. He set his sails, and covered David more warmly, and then lay down under the midnight stars. The wind was at his back, and the lonely land of his birth passed from his eyes as a dream passes. In the morning the islands were not to be seen; they were hidden by belts of phantom foam, wreathed and vexed with spray and spindrift. There was, fortunately, no wrath in the morning tide, only a steady, irresistible set to the westward; and this was just what Liot desired. For many days these favorable circumstances continued, and Liot and David were very happy together; but as they neared the vexed seas which lash Cape Wrath and pour down into the North Minch, Liot had enough to do to keep his boat afloat.

He was driven against his will and way almost to the Butt of Lewis; and as his meal and water were very low, he looked for death in more ways than one. Then the north wind came, and he hoped to reach the broad Bay of Stornoway with it; but it was soon so strong and savage that nothing could be done but make all snug as possible for the gale and then run before it. It proved to be worse than Liot anticipated, and, hungry and thirsty and utterly worn out, the helpless boat and her two dying occupants were picked up by some Celtic coasters from Uig, and taken to the little hamlet to which they were going.

There Liot stayed all summer, fishing with the men of the place; but he was not happy, for, though they were Calvinists as to faith, they were very different from the fair, generous, romantic men of his own islands. For the fishers of Uig were heavy-faced Celts, with the impatient look of men selfish and greedy of gain. They made Liot pay well for such privileges as they gave him; and he looked forward to the close of the fishing season, for then he was determined to go to Stornoway and get David a more comfortable and civilized home, after which he would sell his boat and nets. And then? Then he would take the first passage he could get to Glasgow, for at Glasgow there were ships bound for every port in the world.

It was on the 5th of September that he again set sail for Stornoway, and on the 11th he was once more brought back to Uig. A great storm had stripped him of everything he possessed but his disabled boat. David was in a helpless, senseless condition, and Liot had a broken arm, and fainted from suffering and exhaustion while he was being carried on shore. In some way he lost his purse, and it contained all his money. He looked at the sea and he looked at the men, and he knew not which had it. So there was nothing possible for another winter but poverty and hard toil, and perchance a little hope, now and then, of a better voyage in the spring.

With endless labor and patience he prepared for this third attempt, and one lovely day in early June set sail for the Butt of Lewis. He had good weather and fair winds for two days; then the norther came and drove him round Vatternish, and into the dangerous whirlpools and vexed waterways of that locality. His boat began to leak, and he was forced to abandon her, and for thirty hours to thole the blustering winds and waves that tossed the little cockle-shell, in which they took a last refuge, like a straw upon the billows. Again the men of Uig brought them to shore; and this time they were sulky, and expressed no sympathy for Liot's disappointment, loss, and suffering. They had become superstitious about him, and they speculated and wondered at the ill luck that always drove him back to Skye. Roy Hunish, a very old man, spoke for the rest when he said, "It seems to me, Liot Borson, that the Lord has not sent you to Stornoway; he is against the journey." And Liot answered sadly: "He is against all I desire."

When they had been warmed and fed and rested in one of the nearest cottages, Liot took David in his arms and went back to his old hut. He put the sleeping child in the bunk, and then sat down on the cold, dark hearthstone. What Hunish expressed so plainly was the underlying thought in his own heart. He could not escape from a conclusion so tragically manifested. In sorrow too great for tears, he compelled himself to resign all his hopes and dreams—a renunciation as bitter as wormwood, but not as cruelly bitter as the one it included; for his rejection was also the rejection of his son. God had not forgiven him, nor had he accepted David's dedication to his service, for he had stripped him of all means to accomplish it. He might have permitted him to reach Stornoway and leave the boy among his kindred; he had chosen rather to include David in the sin of his father. This was the thought that wounded his heart like a sword. He went to the sleeping boy and kissed his face, weeping most of all for the sorrow he had brought on the innocent one.

If this earth be a penal world, Liot that night went down to one of its lowest hells. Sorrow of many kinds brutally assailed him. He hid nothing from his consciousness. He compelled himself to see over again the drowning of Bele—that irreparable wrong which had ruined all his happiness; he compelled himself to stand once more by Karen's coffin, and listen to his own voice calling God to witness his innocence; he compelled himself to admit that he had thought God had forgotten his sin of seven years ago. And when these things had been thought out to the end, his heart was so full that he quite unconsciously gave utterance to his thoughts in audible speech. The tones of his voice in the darkness were like those of a man praying, and the hopeless words filled the sorrowful room with a sense of suffering:

"So, then, it is for a life-sentence that I am sent here. There is to be no pardon till I have dreed out the years appointed me in the gust and poverty of this dreadful place, among its hard, unfriendly men. My God! I am but thirty-three years old. How long wilt thou be angry with me? And the little lad! Pass me by, but oh, be merciful to him!"

A great silence followed this imploration. The man was waiting. For hours he sat motionless; but just before dawn he must have heard a word of strength or comfort, for he rose to his feet and bowed his head. He was weeping bitterly, and his voice was like a sob; but from that hut on the wild Skye coast there arose with a heartbroken cry the sublimest of mortal prayers—"*Thy will be done.*"

IV
THE DOOR WIDE OPEN

Resignation is not always contentment, and though Liot accepted God's will in place of his own will, he took it rather with a dour patience than with a cheerful satisfaction. Yet in a certain way life gets made independent of our efforts. A higher power than our own brings events about, finds a way across the hills of difficulty, smooths out the rough places, and makes straight what our folly has made crooked. When it became certain that Liot would make his life-home near Uig the men on that coast began to treat him with more friendliness, and the women pitied and cared a little for his motherless boy. And by and by there came a new minister, who found in Liot a man after his own heart. The two men became familiars, and the friendship made life more supportable to both.

It was a hard existence, however, for the child. Liot loved his son, but he was not a demonstrative father, and he thought more of doing his duty to David than of showing him affection or providing him with pleasure. For when all hopes of making him a minister were over David lost something in Liot's estimation. He was, then, just a common lad, in whose heart, as a matter of course, folly and disobedience were bound up. It was his place to exorcise everything like joy, and with the phantoms of a gloomy creed to darken and terrify his childhood.

Before David had shed his baby teeth, hell and the devil were tremendous realities to him. An immaculate, pitiless God, who delighted in taking vengeance on his enemies, haunted all his boyhood's dreams; and the "scheme of salvation," by which perchance this implacable Deity might be conciliated, was the beginning and the end of his education. With an amazing distinctness in question and answer, this "scheme" was laid before him, and by the word and the rod of admonition he was made familiar with the letter of its awful law.

Here, then, was a child whom a sad destiny had led far away from happiness. His nature was singularly affectionate, yet he had no memory of a mother's kiss, or, indeed, of any tender human kindness. No one petted or loved him; no one heeded his childish sorrows and sufferings. He had toothaches and earaches, about which he felt it useless to speak. He went into the boats with his father as soon as he could bait a line, and was forced to endure all that men endured from salt-water boils, chilblains, frost-bites, and the lashing of spray-laden winds. Cold and hunger, heat and thirst, and the frequent intolerable sleepiness of overtaxed strength made up the sad drama of his childhood; and he played his part in it with a patient submission that sometimes won from his father astonishment and a few words of praise or admiration.

Such words made glorious epochs in the boy's life; he could remember every one of them. Once, when Liot could get no one to launch a boat and go with him to the help of four men drowning before their eyes, the ten-year-old lad came radiantly forward and said, "Take me, father; I will go with you." And the two went on the desperate errand together, and brought back safely the men ready to perish. Then, when all was well over and the child stood trembling with exhaustion, Liot drew him close to his side, and pushed his wet hair from his brow, and said with proud tenderness, "You are a good, brave boy. God bless you, David!" And the happy upward look of the child had his mother's smile in it, and before Liot knew what he was doing he had stooped and kissed him. The event was a wonderful one, and it made a tie between the father and the son that it was beyond the power of time to loosen.

Liot's own boyhood had been filled with the dreams and stories of the elder world. He had been conscious all his life of this influence streaming up from the centuries behind him, and coloring, and even moving, his present existence. The fierce hatred he felt for Bele Trenby came from unchristened ancestors, and the dumb murder, which had darkened his life and sent him to Uig, from the same source. He told David none of these stirring sagas. He was resolved that the knowledge of the thrall's curse should not call sorrow to him. He never named the heroic Gisli in his hearing. And once, when he found an old fisherman reciting "Ossian" to David, he fell into such anger as terrified every one. Indeed, he said words at that hour which would have made much trouble and ill-will if the minister had not justified them and called Liot's anger a "righteous one."

And in those days there was absolutely no literature for the people. Books were dear and scarce; ten years might pass without a new one drifting into a hamlet; and newspapers were few and for the rich alone. David, then, had but one book–the Holy Scriptures. He read them, and read them again, and found everything in them. Fortunately, the wonderful wisdom and stories of the Apocrypha had not then been discarded; the book had its place between the Old and the New Testament. And David was wise with Solomon, and saw beautiful visions with Esdras, and lived and glowed and fought with the heroic Maccabees.

And we who have far more books than we can read can hardly understand how David loved the Bible. It was his poetry, his philosophy, his history; it was, above all, the speech of God to man. Through it he breathed the air of the old, old East, and grew up under the shadows of Judea's palms and olives; so that the rainy gloom of the coast of Skye was but an accident of his existence. Abraham and Joseph, Moses and Joshua, were far more real personages to David Borson than the Duke of Wellington or Napoleon and his twelve marshals. Through the stormy days when it was impossible to go to sea, and in the long winter nights, when he stretched himself before the red peats with a little oil-cruse, he and the Bible were friends and companions. It kept him in direct relation with God and heaven; it fed him on faith; it made him subject to duty; it gave him a character at once courageous and gentle, calm and ideal—such a character as is very rare in our days, and which, where it does exist, will *not* be transmitted.

So that, with all his hard work and many deprivations, David had his happy hours. And the years went by, and he grew up to a fair and stately manhood, not rebelling against his fate, but taking it as a part of the inscrutable mystery of life and death constantly before his eyes. Others around him suffered in like manner, and at the end one thing happened to all. No; it was not the tyranny of nature nor of his material life that troubled David as he approached manhood; it was the spiritual tyranny under which he lived and prayed which darkened his days and filled his nights with thoughts which he dared not follow to their proper conclusion and was equally afraid to dismiss.

This was his dilemma. He had been taught by a father whom he trusted implicitly that life was only a short and precarious opportunity for working out his salvation with fear and trembling; peradventure he might be counted among the remnant whom God would elect to save from eternal misery. And in a measure the constant east winds and cloudy heavens, the cold and stormy seas, and the gloom and poverty of all his surroundings were so many confirmations of this unhappy conviction. Yet it was very hard for him to believe that the God of the Bible, "like a father pitying his children," was the God of his Shorter and Longer Catechisms. As his twentieth year approached these doubts and questions would not be put away, and yet he dared not speak of them either to the minister or to his father.

Then, one night, as he was watching his lines and hooks, something happened which broke the adamantine seal upon his soul. He was quite alone in his boat, and she was drifting slowly under the full moon; there was not a sound upon the ocean but the wash of the water against her sides. He was sitting motionless, thinking of the sadness and weariness of life, and wishing that God would love him, though ever so little, and, above all, that he would give him some word or sign of his care for him. His hands were clasped upon his knees, his eyes fixed on the far horizon; between him and the God whom he so ignorantly feared and desired there was apparently infinite space and infinite silence.

All at once some one seemed to come into the boat beside him. An ineffable peace and tenderness, a sweetness not to be described, encompassed the lonely youth. He was sensible of a glory he could not see; he was comforted by words that were inaudible to his natural ears. During this transitory experience he scarcely breathed, but as it slowly passed away he rose reverently to his feet. "An angel has been with me," he thought.

After this event the whole fabric of his creed vanished at times before the inexplicable revelation. Yet the terrible power of early impressions is not easily eradicated, even by the supernatural; and whenever he reasoned about the circumstance he came to the conclusion that it might have been a snare and a delusion of the Evil One. For why should an angel be sent with a word to him? or why should he dare to hope that his longing after God's love had touched the heart of the Eternal? Yet, though the glory was dissolved by the doubting, nothing could quite rob him of his blessing; in the midst of the sternest realities of his rough daily toil he found himself musing on those wonderful days when angels went and came among men as they threshed their wheat or worked at their handicrafts, when prayer was visibly answered and the fire dropped from heaven on the accepted sacrifice.

He thought the more on this subject because his father was visibly dying from some internal disease, which was dissolving with rapid, inexorable suffering the house of clay in which the soul of Liot Borson dwelt. Liot was aware of it, and had borne with silent courage the enemy's advances toward the citadel of life. Very reluctantly he had given up his duties one by one, until the day came when nothing remained for him to do but to wait and to suffer; then he spoke plainly to David. It happened to be the lad's twenty-sixth birthday, and Liot had his own memories of the first one. Almost inadvertently the name of Karen passed his lips, and then he talked long of her goodness, her love, and her beauty; and David listened with an interest that tempted more confidence than Liot had ever thought to give.

"If you had such a wife as Karen Sabiston was to me," he said, "then, David, you would be happy even in this place. But you will not stay here. When I am gone away to the land very far off, then you will go back to Shetland–to your own land and your own people."

"I will do as you wish, father."

"You will marry; that is to be looked for. I have seen that girl of Talisker's watching you, and luring you with her sly smiles and glances. Give her no notice. I like not these Celtic women, with their round black eyes and their red color and black hair. In Shetland you will see women that you may safely love–good and beautiful girls of your own race; there must be no strange women among the Borsons. Your Bible tells you what sorrow comes from marrying daughters of Heth and their like. Go to Shetland for your wife."

"I will, father."

"You will find friends and kindred there—my good cousin Paul, and his sons and daughters, and your mother's family in Yell, and Matilda Sabiston. I would say something of her, but she is doubtless in the grave by this time, and gone to the mercy of the Merciful."

"Was she of our kindred, then?"

"Of your mother's kin. They were ill friends here, but yonder all may—all *will* be different."

During this conversation Liot made his son understand that the messenger of release might come at any hour; but in the morning he felt so free from pain that David thought he could safely go to the early fishing. When he reached the pier, however, the boat had sailed without him, and he walked into Uig and told the minister how near the end it was. And the minister answered:

"We have had our farewell, David. We shall meet no more till we meet in the city of God." He spoke with a subdued enthusiasm, and his grave face was luminous with an interior transfiguration. Suddenly the sun came from behind a cloud, and the flying shower was crowned with a glorious rainbow. He drew David to the window, and said in a rapture of adoration:

"The token of His covenant! It compasseth the heavens about with a glorious circle, and *the hands of the Most High have bended it*. Could any words be more vitally realistic, David? Tell your father what you have seen—the token of His covenant! The token of His covenant!"

And David went away, awed and silent; for there was in the minister's eyes that singular brilliance which presages a vision of things invisible. They looked straight into the sunshine. Did they see beyond it to where the "innumerable company of angels" were singing, "Holy, holy, holy"?

Indeed, he was so much impressed that he took the longest way home. He wanted to think over what his father and the minister had said, and he wanted that solitude of nature which had so often been to him the voice of God. The road itself was only a foot-path across a melancholy moor, covered with heather and boulders, and encompassed by cyclopean wrecks of mountains, the vapory outlines of which suggested nothing but endless ruin. Although the season was midsummer, there had been sharp, surly whiffs of rain all day long, and the dreary levels were full of little lochs of black moss water. So David kept to the seaward side, where the land was higher, and where he could see the roll of a spent gale swinging round

Vatternish toward the red, rent bastions of Skye, and hear its thunder amid the purple caves of the basalt and the whitened tiers of the oölite, silencing all meaner sounds.

After a trailing, thoughtful walk of a mile, he came to a spot where a circle of druidical monoliths stood huge and pale in the misty air. He went straight into the haunted place with the manner of one familiar with it, cast his nets on the low central stone which had once been the sacrificial altar of the dead creed, and then leaned wearily against one of the sheltering pillars.

His person was at this time remarkably handsome and in wonderful harmony with its surroundings. He was large and strong—a man not made for the narrow doorways of the town, but for the wide, stormy spaces of the unstreeted ocean. The sea was in his eyes, which were blue and outlooking; his broad breast was bared to the wind and rain; his legs were planted apart, as if he was hauling up an anchor or standing on a reeling deck. An air of somber gravity, a face sad and mystical, distinguished his solitary figure. He was the unconscious incarnation of the lonely land and the stormy sea.

Leaning against the pagan pillar, he revolved in his mind those great questions that survive every change of race and dynasty: Whence come we? Where go we? How can a man be justified with God? Though the rain smote him east and west, he was in the sunshine of the Holy Land; he was drawing nets with Simon Peter on the Sea of Galilee; he was listening to Him who spake as never man spake. Suddenly the sharp whistle of a passing steamer roused him. He turned his eyes seaward, and saw the *Polly Ann* hastening to the railway port with her load of fish for the Glasgow market. The sight set him again in the nineteenth century. Then he felt the rain, and he drew his bonnet over his brows, and lifted his nets, and began to walk toward the little black hut on the horizon. It was of large stones roughly mortared together, and it had a low chimney, and a door fastened with a leather strap; but the small window wanted the screen of white muslin usual in Highland cots, and was dim with dust and cobwebs.

It was David's home, and he knew his father waited there for his coming; so he hastened his steps; but the radiant, dreamy look which had made him handsome was gone, and he approached the door with the air of a man who is weary of to-day and without hope for the morrow. At the threshold he threw off this aspect, and entered with a smile. His father, sitting wearily in a wooden arm-chair, turned his face to meet him. It was the face of a man walking with death. Human agony grimly borne without complaint furrowed it; gray as ashes were the cheeks, and the eyes alone retained the "spark of heavenly flame" which we call life.

"There has been a change, David," he said, "and it is well you are come; for I know I must soon be going, and there is this and that to say—as there always is at the parting."

"I see that you are worse, father. Let me go for the doctor now."

"I will have no man meddle with the hour of my death; no one shall either hurry or delay it."

"The doctor might give you some ease from your sore pain."

"I will bear His will to the uttermost. But come near to me, David; I have some last words to say, and there is One at my side hasting me forward."

"Tell me your wish now, father. I will do all that you desire."

"When you have put me in my grave, go to Shetland for me. I thought to do my own errand—to get there just in time to do it, and die; but it is hard counting with Death—he comes sooner than you expect. David, I have brought you up in the way of life. Think no wrong of me when I am gone away forever. Indeed, you'll not dare to," he said with a sudden flash of natural pride in himself; "for though I may have had a sore downfall, I could not get away from His love and favor."

"None living shall say wrong of you in my hearing, father."

"But, David, there are those of the unregenerate who would make much of my little slip. I might die, lad, and say nothing to any man about it. Put a few peats on the fire; death is cold, and my feet are in the grave already; so I may tell the truth now, for at this hour no man can make me afraid. And there is no sin, I hope, in letting Matilda Sabiston know, if she is still alive, that I owe Bele Trenby nothing for the wrong he did me. St. Paul left the Almighty to pay the ill-will he owed Alexander the coppersmith; but I could not ask that much favor, being only Liot Borson; and no doubt the Lord suffered me to pay my own debt—time and place being put so unexpected into my hand."

Then he was awfully silent. The mortal agony was dealing its last sharp blows, and every instinct impelled him to cry out against the torment. But Liot Borson had put his mortality beneath his feet; nothing could have forced a cry from him. His face changed as a green leaf might change if a hot iron was passed over it; but he sat grasping the rude arms of his wooden chair, disdaining the torture while it lasted, and smiling triumphantly as it partly passed away.

"A few more such pangs and the fight will be over, David. So I will swither and scruple no longer; I will tell the whole truth about the drowning of Bele Trenby. Bele and I were never friends; but I hated him when he began to meddle between me and Karen Sabiston. He had no shadow of right to do so, for I had set my heart on her and she had given me her promise; and I said then, and I say it now with death at my elbow, that he had no right to step between me and Karen. Yet he tried to do that thing, and if it had not been for the minister I had stabbed him to his false heart. But the minister bade me do no wrong, because I was of the household of faith, and a born and baptized child of God, having come—mind this, David—of generations of his saints. He said if Bele had done me wrong, wrong would come to Bele, and I would live to see it."

"'Vengeance is Mine; I will repay'," quoted David, in a low voice. But Liot answered sharply:

"The Lord sends by whom he will send. And it so happened that one night, as Bele and I were walking together, I knew the hour had come."

"You took not the matter in your own hands surely, father?"

"There was none there but me. I laid no finger on him; he fell into his own snare. I had said a thousand times—and the Lord had heard me say it—that if one word of mine would save Bele Trenby from death, I would not say that one word. Could I break my oath for a child of the Evil One? Had Bele been of the elect I would have borne that in mind; but Bele came of bad stock; pirates and smugglers were his forebears, and the women not to name with the God-fearing—light and vain women. So I hated Bele, and I had a right to hate him; and one night, as I walked from Quarf to Lerwick, Bele came to my side and said, 'Good evening, Liot.' And I said, 'It is dark,' and spoke no more. And by and by we came to a stream swollen with rain and snow-water, and Bele said, 'Here is the crossing.' And I answered him not, for I knew it was *not* the crossing. So as I delayed a little—for my shoe-string was loose—Bele said again, 'Here is the crossing.' And I told him neither yes nor no. And he said to me, 'It seemeth, Liot, thou art in a devil's temper, and I will stay no longer with thee.' And with the ill words on his lips he strode into the stream, and then overhead into the moss he went, and so to his own place."

"Father, I am feared for a thing like that. There would be sin in it."

"I lifted no finger against him; my lips lied not. It was the working out of his own sin that slew him."

"I would have warned him—yes, I would. Let me go for the minister; he will not be feared to say, 'Liot, you did wrong,' if so he thinks."

"I have had my plea out with my Maker. If I did sin, I have paid the price of the sin. Your mother was given to me, and in two years the Lord took her away. I thought to fill my eyes with a sight of the whole world, and I was sent to this desolate place for a life-sentence, to bide its storm and gloom and gust and poverty, and in this bit cabin to dree a long, fierce wrestle with Death, knowing all the time he would get the mastery over me in the end." Then, suddenly pausing, his gray face glowed with passionate rapture, and lifting up his right hand he cried out: "No, no, David; *I* am the conqueror! There are two ways of dying, my lad–victory and defeat. Thank God, I have the victory through Jesus Christ, my Lord and Saviour!"

"Who is the propitiation for all sin, father."

"Sin!" cried the dying man, "sin! I have nothing to do with sin. 'Who shall lay anything to the charge of God's elect?' for, 'Whosoever is born of God doth not commit sin–he cannot sin, for he is born of God.' I did indeed make a sore stumble; so also did David, and natheless he was a man after God's own heart. What has man to do with my fault? *He* has entered into judgment with me, and I have gladly borne the hand of the smiter."

"Gladly, father?"

"Ay, David, gladly. For had I not been *his* son, he would have 'let me alone,' as he does those joined to their idols; but because he loved me he chastised me; and I have found that his rod as well as his staff can comfort in affliction. Some of his bairns deserve and get the rod of iron. Be good, David, and he will stretch out to you only his golden scepter."

"And also you have the Intercessor."

"If I had not I would plead my own cause, as Job did. I would rise up and answer him like a man, for he is a just God. Mercy may have times and seasons, but justice is the same yesterday, to-day, and forever. 'Shall not the Judge of all the earth do right?'"

"Would you say that, father, if justice sent you to the place of torment?"

"Ay, would I! 'Though he slay me, yet will I trust in him.' But I am not fearing the place of torment, David. And as for this world, it is at my feet like a cast-off shoe, and all its gold and gear is as the wrack of the sea. But you will find a few sovereigns in my chest, and a letter for your cousin Paul Borson; and the ship and the house you may do your will with."

"It is your will in all things that I care to do, father. And now, if you would but let me away for the minister, maybe you could say a word to him you are not caring to say to me–a word of sorrow or remorse–"

"Remorse! remorse! No, no, David! Remorse is for feeble souls; remorse is the virtue of hell; remorse would sin again if it could. I have repented, David, and repentance ends all. See to your Larger Catechism, David– Question ."

Throughout this conversation speech had been becoming more and more painful to him. The last words were uttered in gasps of unconquerable agony, and a mortal spasm gave a terrible emphasis to this spiritual conviction. When it had passed he whispered faintly, "The pains of hell get hold on me—on my body, David; they cannot touch my soul. Lay me down now—at His feet—I can sit in my chair no longer."

So David laid him in his bunk. "Shall I say *the words* now—the words you marked, father?" he asked.

"Ay; the hour has come."

Then David knelt down and put his young, fresh face very close to the face of the dying man, and said solemnly and clearly in his very ear the chosen words of trust:

"When the waves of death compassed me;

"When the sorrows of hell compassed me about, and the snares of death prevented me,

"In my distress I called upon the Lord, and cried to my God: and he did hear my voice out of his temple, and my cry did enter into his ears."

<hr size=2 width="40%" align=center>

"The sorrows of death compassed me, and the pains of hell gat hold upon me: I found trouble and sorrow.

"Then called I upon the name of the Lord; O Lord, I beseech thee, deliver my soul....

"Return unto thy rest, O my soul; for the Lord hath dealt bountifully with thee.

"For thou hast delivered my soul from death, mine eyes from tears, and my feet from falling....

"Precious in the sight of the Lord is the death of his saints."

Here David ceased. It was evident that the mighty words were no longer necessary. A smile, such as is never seen on mortal face until the light of eternity falls upon it, illumined the gaunt, stern features, and the outlooking eyes flashed a moment in its radiance. A solemn calm, a certain pomp of conscious grandeur in his victory over death and the grave, encompassed the dying man, and gave to the prone figure a majestic significance. As far as this world was concerned, Liot Borson was a dead man. For two days he lingered on life's outermost shoal, but at sunrise the third morning he went silently away. It was full tide; the waves broke softly on the shingle, and the sea-birds on the lonely rocks were crying for their meat from God.

Suddenly the sunshine filled the cabin, and David was aware of something more than the morning breeze coming through the wide-open door. A sense of lofty *presence* filled the place. "It is the flitting," he said with a great awe; and he stood up with bowed head until a feeling of indescribable loneliness testified that the soul which had hitherto dwelt with him was gone away forever.

He went then to the body. Death had given it dignity and grandeur. It was evident that in Liot's case the great change had meant victory and not defeat. Almost for the first time in his life David kissed his father. Then he went into Uig and told the minister, and said simply to his mates, "My father is dead." And they answered:

"It is a happy change for him, David. Is it to-morrow afternoon you would like us to come?"

And David said: "Yes; at three o'clock the minister will be there."

He declined all companionship; he could wake alone with the dead. For the most part he sat on the door-step and watched the rising and setting of the constellations, or walked to and fro before the open door, ever awfully aware of that outstretched form, the house of clay in which his father and companion had dwelt so many years at his side. Sometimes he slept a little with his head against the post of the door, and then the sudden waking in the starlight made him tremble.

He had thought this night would be a session of solemnity never to be forgotten; but he found himself dozing and his thoughts drifting, and it was only by an effort that he could compel anything like the attitude he desired. For we cannot kindle when we will the sacred fire of the soul. And David was disappointed in his spiritual experience, and shocked at what he called his coldness and indifference, which, after all, were not coldness and indifference, but the apathy of exhausted feeling and physical weariness.

The next afternoon there was a quiet gathering in the cabin that had been Liot's, and a little prayer and admonition; then, in the beauteous stillness of the summer day, the fishers made a bier of their crossed oars, and David laid his father upon it. There was no coffin; the long, majestic figure of humanity was only folded close in a winding-sheet and his own blue blanket. So, by the sea-shore, as the tide murmured and the sun glinted brightly through swirling banks of gray clouds, they carried him to his long home. No one spoke as he entered it. The minister dropped his kerchief upon the upturned face, and David cast the first earth. Then the dead man's friends, each taking the spade in his turn, filled in the empty place, and laid over it the sod, and went silently away in twos and threes, each to his own home.

When all had disappeared, David followed. He had now an irresistible impulse to escape from his old surroundings. He did not feel as if he cared to see again any one who had been a part of his past. He went back to the cabin, ate some bread and fish, and then with a little reluctance opened his father's chest. There was small wealth in it—only some letters, and Liot's kirk clothes, and a leather purse containing sixteen sovereigns. David saw at a glance that the letters were written by his mother. He wondered a moment if his father had yet found her again, and then he kissed the bits of faded script and laid them upon the glowing peats. The money he put in his pocket, and the chest and clothing he resolved to take to Shetland with him. As for the cabin, he decided to give it to Bella Campbell. "She was sore put to it last winter to shelter her five fatherless bairns; and if my father liked any one more than others, it was Angus Campbell," he thought.

Then he went out and looked at the boat. "It is small," he said, "but it will carry me to Shetland. I can keep in the shadows of the shore. And though it is a far sail round Cape Wrath and Dunnet Head, it is summer weather, and I'll win my way if it so pleases God."

And thus it happened that on the first day of August this lonely wayfarer on cheerless seas caught sight of the gray cliffs of the Shetlands, lying like dusky spots in the sapphire and crimson splendors of the setting sun.

---

ly
Book Second

V
A NEW LIFE

Between David and the misty Hebrides there was now many a league of the separating, changeful, dangerous, tragic sea, but the journey over this great waterway had been a singularly fortunate one. David, indeed, had frequently likened himself to the young Tobias on a similar errand; for his father had particularly pointed out this history, and had read aloud to him with an emphasis not to be forgotten the old Hebrew father's parting charge: "Go! and God, which dwelleth in heaven, prosper your journey, and the angel of God keep you company."

To David this angelic companionship was no impossible hope and reliance. As the south winds drove him north and the west winds sent him east just at the proper times, he believed that some wise and powerful pilot stood at the wheel unseen; and he went about his boat with the cheerful confidence of a child who is sure his father can take care of him. Sometimes he kept so close to the shore that he rippled the shadows of the great cliffs, and sometimes he ran into little coves and replenished his water-casks, or bought in the seaward clachans a supply of fresh cakes or fish. He met no very bad weather. The unutterable desolation of the misty miles of sullen water did give him times of such weariness as makes the soul sink back upon itself and retire from all hope and affection. But such hours were evanescent; they were usually ended by a brisk wind, bringing peril to the little bark, and then David's first instinct was heavenward. He knew if the winds and waves rose mightily, as it was their wont in that locality, there was no human help, and his trust was instantly in the miraculous. Such hours were, however, rare. As a general thing the days and the nights followed each other with a stillness and beauty full of the presence of God. And in the sweetness of this presence he threw himself unperplexed upon infinite love and power, and seeking God with all his heart found him.

Also, he was not forgetful of the human interest of his journey. His father had always felt himself to be a stranger and an exile in Skye, and in his later years the "homing" instinct for the Shetlands had been a passionate longing, which had communicated itself to David. He had been glad to leave Uig, for he had not a single happy memory of the little hut in which they two had dwelt and suffered together. As for the bleak kirkyard, over which the great winds blew the sea-foam, it made his heart ache to remember it. He felt an unspeakable pity when he thought of one of its solitary graves, and he promised himself to sail back to Uig some day, and bring home the dust of his father, and lay it among his kindred.

Indeed, it was thoughts of home and kindred which made this long, lonely voyage happy and hopeful to David. He believed himself to be going home. Though his father at the last had not spoken much of his cousin Paul Borson, and though David had not found the letter which was to be his introduction to him, yet he had not a doubt of his welcome. Time might wither friendship and slay love, but his kindred were always his kindred; they were bound to him by the ineffaceable and imperishable ties of blood and race.

David approached Lerwick in that divine twilight which in the Shetland summer links day unto day; and in its glory the ancient homes of gray and white sandstone appeared splendid habitations. The town was very quiet; even the houses seemed to be asleep. He saw no living thing but a solitary sea-gull skimming the surface of the sea; he heard nothing but a drunken sailor fitfully singing a stave of "The Skaalds of Foula." The clear air, the serene seas, the tranquil grandeur of the caverned rocks which guard the lonely isles, charmed him. And when the sun rose and he saw their mural fronts of porphyry, carved by storms into ten thousand castles in the air, and cloud-like palaces still more fantastic, he felt his heart glow for the land of his birth and the home of his forefathers.

To the tumult of almost impossible hopes, he brought in his little craft. He had felt certain that his appearance would awaken at once interest and speculation; that Paul Borson would hear of his arrival and come running to meet him; that his father's old friends, catching the news, would stop him on the quay and the street, and ask him questions and give him welcome. He had also told himself that it was likely his father's cousin would have sons and daughters, and if so, that they would certainly be glad to see him; besides which there was his mother's family—the old Icelandic Sabistons. He was resolved to seek them all out, rich or poor, far or near; in his heart there was love enough and to spare, however distant the kinship might be.

For David's conceptions of the family and racial tie were not only founded upon the wide Hebraic ideals, but his singularly lonely youth and affectionate nature had disposed him to make an exaggerated estimate of the obligations of kindred. And again, this personal leaning was greatly strengthened by the inherited tendency of Norse families to "stand by each other in all haps." Therefore he felt sure of his welcome; for, though Paul was but his far-off cousin, they were both Borsons, sprung from the same Norse root, children of the same great ancestor, the wise and brave Norwegian Bor.

Lying in the Bay of Lerwick, the sense of security and of nearness to friends gave him what he had long missed—a night of deep, dreamless sleep. When he awoke it was late in the morning, and he had his breakfast to prepare and every spar and sail and rope to put in perfect order; then he dressed himself with care, and sailed into harbor, managing his boat with a deftness and skill he expected a town of fishermen and sailors to take notice of. Alas, it is so difficult to find a fortunate hour! David's necessary delay had brought the morning nearly to the noon, and he could hardly have fallen on a more depressing time; for the trade of the early morning was over, and the men were in their houses taking that sleep which those who work by night must secure in the daytime. The fishing-boats, all emptied of their last night's "take" and cleaned, were idly rocking on the water. The utmost quiet reigned in the sunny streets, and the little pier was deserted. No one took any notice of David.

Greatly disappointed, and even wounded, by this very natural neglect, David made fast his boat and stepped on shore. He put his feet down firmly, as if he was taking possession of his own, and stood still and looked around. He saw a man with his hands in his pockets loitering down the street, and he went toward him; but as he came within speaking distance the man turned into a house and shut the door. Pained and curious, he continued his aimless walk. As he passed Fae's store he heard the confused sound of a number of men talking, then silence, then the tingling notes of a fiddle very cleverly played. For a moment he was bewitched by the music; then he was sure that nothing but the little sinful fiddle of carnal dance and song could make sounds so full of temptation. And as Odysseus, passing the dwelling-place of the sirens, "closed his ears and went swiftly by, singing the praises of the gods," so David, remembering his father's counsels, closed his ears to the enchanting strains and hastened beyond their power to charm him.

A little farther on a lovely girl, with her water-pitcher on her head and her knitting in her hands, met him. She looked with a shy smile at David, and the glance from her eyes made him thrill with pleasure; but before he had a word ready she had passed, and he could only turn and look at her tall form and the heavy braids of pale-brown hair below the water-pitcher. He felt as if he were in a dream as he went onward again down the narrow street of gray and white houses–houses so tall, and so fantastic, and so much larger than he had ever seen, that they impressed him with a sense of grandeur in which he had neither right nor place; for, though he saw women moving about within them and children sitting on the door-steps, no one spoke to him, no one seemed interested in his presence; and yet he had come to them with a heart so full of love! Never for a moment did he reflect that his anticipations had rested only on his own desires and imaginations.

His disappointment made him sorrowful, but in no degree resentful. "It was not to be," he decided. Then he resolved to return to a public house he had noticed by the pier. There he could get his dinner and make some inquiries about his kindred. As he turned he met face to face a middle-aged woman with a basket of turf on her back.

"Take care, my lad," she said cheerfully; and her smile inspired David with confidence.

"Mother," he said, doffing his cap with instinctive politeness, "mother, I am a stranger, and I want to find my father's people–the Borsons. Where do they live?"

"My lad, the sea has them. It is Paul Borson you are asking for?"

"Yes, mother."

"He went out in his boat with his four sons one night. The boat came back empty. It is two years since."

"'I WANT TO FIND MY FATHER'S PEOPLE.'"

"I am Liot Borson's son."

"You?"

"Yes. Have I any kin left?"

"There is your far-cousin Nanna. She was Paul's one daughter, and he saw the sun shine through her eyes. She is but sadly off now. Come into my house, and I will give you a cup of tea and a mouthful of bread and fish. Thank God, there is enough for you and for me!"

"I will come," said David, simply; and he took the basket from the woman, and flung it lightly over his own shoulder. Then they went together to a house in one of the numerous "closes" running from the main street to the ocean. It was a very small house, but it was clean, and was built upon a rock, the foundations of which were deep down in the sea. When the tide was full David could have sailed his boat under its small seaward window. It contained a few pieces of handsome furniture, and some old Delft earthenware which had been brought from Holland by seafaring kindred long ago; all else savored of narrow means.

But the woman set before David a pot of tea and some oat-cake, and she fried him a fresh herring, and he ate with the delayed hunger of healthy youth, heartily and with pleasure. And as he did so she talked to him of his father Liot, whom she had known in her girlhood; and David told her of Liot's long, hard fight with death, and she said with a kind of sad pride:

"Yes; that way Liot was sure to fare to his long home. He would set his teeth and fight for his life. Was it always well between him and you?"

"He was hard and silent, but I could always lean on him as much as I liked."

"That is a good deal to say."

"So I think."

Then they drew the past from the eternity into which it had fallen, that they two, brought so strangely together, might look at it between them. They talked of Liot's hard life and hard death for an hour, and then the woman said:

"Paul Borson was of the same kind—silent, but full of deeds; and his daughter Nanna, she also has a great heart."

"Show me now where she lives, and I will go and see her. Also, tell me your name."

"I am Barbara Traill. When you have seen Nanna come back here, and I will give you a place to sleep and a little meat; and as soon as it is well with you it will be easy to pay my charges."

"If there is no room for me in my cousin's house I will come back to you."

So Barbara walked with him to the end of the street, and pointed out a little group of huts on the distant moor.

"Go into the first one," she said; "it is Nanna Sinclair's. And be sure and keep to the trodden path, for outside of it there are bogs that no man knows the bottom of."

Then David went forward alone, and his heart fell, and a somber look crept like a cloud over his face. This was not the home-coming he had anticipated—this poor meal at a stranger's fireside. He had been led to think that his cousin Paul had a large house and the touch of money-getting. "He and his will be well off," Liot had affirmed more than once. And one day, while he yet could stand in the door of his hut, he had looked longingly northward and said, "Oh, if I could win home again! Paul would make a fourteen days' feast to welcome me."

The very vagueness of these remarks had given strength to David's imagination. He had hoped for things larger than his knowledge, and he had quite forgotten to take into his calculations the fact that as the years wear on they wear out love and life, and leave little but graves behind them. At this hour he felt his destiny to be hard and unlovely, and the text learned as one of the pillars of his faith, "Jacob have I loved, Esau have I hated," forced itself upon his reflection. A deadly fear came into his heart that the Borsons were among these hated ones. Why else did God pursue them with such sufferings and fatalities? And what could he do to propitiate this unfriendly Deity?

His road was upon the top of the cliff, over a moor covered with peat-bogs and withered heather. The sea was below him, and a long, narrow lake lay silent and motionless among the dangerous moss—a lake so old and dead-looking that it might have been the shadow of a lake that once was. Nothing green was near it, and no birds were tempted by its sullen waters; yet untold myriads of sea-birds floated and wheeled between sea and sky, and their hungry, melancholy cries and the desolate landscape stimulated and colored David's sad musings, though he was quite unaware of their influence.

When he came to the group of huts, he paused a moment. They were the abodes of poverty; there was none better than the rest. But Barbara had said that Nanna's was the first one, and he went slowly toward it. No one appeared, though the door stood wide open; but when he reached the threshold he could see Nanna sitting within. She was busily braiding the fine Tuscan straw for which Shetland was then famous, and her eyes were so intently following her rapid fingers that it was unlikely she had seen him coming. Indeed, she did not raise them at once, for it was necessary to leave her work at a certain point; and in that moment's delay David looked with a breathless wonder at the woman before him.

She was sitting, and yet even sitting she was majestic. Her face was large, but perfectly oval, and fair as a lily; her bright-brown hair was parted, passed smoothly behind the ears, and beautifully braided. Serenity and an unalterable calm gave to the young face something of the fixity of marble; but as David spoke she let her eyes fall upon a little child at her feet, and then lifted them to him with a smile as radiant and life-giving as sunshine.

"Who are you?" she asked, as she took her babe in her arms and went toward David.

"I am your far-cousin David Borson."

"The son of my father's cousin Liot?"

"Yes. Liot Borson is dead, and here am I."

"You are welcome, for you were to come. My father talked often of his cousin Liot. They are both gone away from this world."

"I think they have found each other again. Who can tell?"

"Among the great multitude that no man can number, it might not be easy."

"If God willed it so?"

"That would be sufficient. This is your little cousin Vala; she is nearly two years old. Is she not very pretty?"

"I know not what to say. She is too pretty for words."

"Sit down, cousin, and tell me all."

And as they talked her eyes enthralled him. They were deep blue, and had a solar brilliancy as if they imbibed light—holy eyes, with the slow-moving pupils that indicate a religious, perhaps a mystical, soul. David sat with her until sunset, and she gave him a simple meal of bread and tea, and talked confidentially to him of Liot and of her own father and brothers. But of herself she said nothing at all; neither could David find courage to ask her a single question.

He watched her sing her child to sleep, and he sat down with her on the door-step, and they talked softly together of death and of judgment to come. And the women from the other huts gradually joined them, and the soft Shetland night glorified the somber land and the mysterious sea, until at last David rose and said he must go back to Lerwick, for the day was over.

A strange day it had been to him; but he was too primitive to attempt any reasoning about its events. When he left Nanna's he was under that strong excitement which makes a man walk as if he were treading upon the void, and there was a hot confusion in his thoughts and feelings. He stepped rapidly, and the stillness of the lovely night did not soothe or reason with him. As he approached the town he saw the fishing-boats leaving the harbor, and in the fairy light they looked like living things with outspread wings. Two fishers were standing at a house door with a woman, who was filling a glass. She held it aloft a moment, and then gave it to one with the words: "Death to the heads that wear no hair!"

"The herring and the halibut, the haddock and the sole," answered the man; and he drank a little, and passed it to his comrade. Then up the street they hurried like belated men; and David felt the urging of accustomed work, and a sense of delinquency in his purposeless hands.

He found Barbara waiting. She knew that he would not stay at Nanna Sinclair's, and she had prepared the room of her absent son for him. "If he can pay one shilling a day, it will be a godsend to me," she thought; and when she told David so he answered, "That is a little matter, and no doubt there will be good between us."

He saw then that the window was open, and the sea-water lippering nearly to the sill of it; and he took off his bonnet, and sat down, and let the cool breeze blow upon his hot brow. It was near midnight, but what then? David had never been more awake in all his life—yes, awake to his finger-tips. Yet for half an hour he sat by the window and never opened his mouth; and Barbara sat on the hearth, and raked the smoldering peats together, and kept a like silence. She was well used to talk with her own thoughts, and to utter words was no necessity to Barbara Traill; but she knew what David was thinking of, and she was quite prepared for the first word which parted his set lips.

"Is my cousin Nanna a widow?"

"No."

"Where, then, is her husband?"

"Who can tell? He is gone away from Shetland, and no one is sorry for that."

"One thing is sure—Nanna is poor, and she is in trouble. How comes that? Who is to blame in the matter?"

"Nicol Sinclair—he, and he only. Sorrow and suffering and ill luck of all kinds he has brought her, and there is no help for it."

"No help for it! I shall see about that."

"You had best let Nicol Sinclair alone. He is one of the worst of men, a son of the devil—no, the very devil himself. And he has your kinswoman Matilda Sabiston at his back. All the ill he does to Nanna he does to please her. To be sure, the guessing is not all that way, but yet most people think Matilda is much to blame."

"How came Nanna Borson to marry such a man? Was not her father alive? Had she no brothers to stand between her and this son of the Evil One?"

"When Nanna Borson took hold of Nicol Sinclair for a husband she thought she had taken hold of heaven; and he was not unkind to her until after the drowning of her kin. Then he took her money and traded with it to Holland, and lost it all there, and came back bare and empty-handed. And when he entered his home there was the baby girl, and Nanna out of her mind with fever and like to die, and not able to say a word this way or that. And Nicol wanted money, and he went to Matilda Sabiston and he got what he wanted; but what was then said no one knows, for ever since he has hated the Borsons, root and branch, and his own wife and child have borne the weight of it. That is not all."

"Tell me all, then; but make no more of it than it is worth."

"There is little need to do that. Before Nanna was strong again he sold the house which Paul Borson had given to her as a marriage present. He sold also all the plenishing, and whatever else he could lay his hands on. Then he set sail; but there was little space between two bad deeds, for no sooner was he home again than he took the money Paul Borson had put in the bank for his daughter, and when no one saw him–in the night-time–he slipped away with a sound skin, the devil knows where he went to."

"Were there no men in Lerwick at that time?"

"Many men were in Lerwick–men, too, who never get to their feet for nothing; and no man was so well hated as Nicol Sinclair. But Nanna said: 'I have had sorrow enough. If you touch him you touch me ten-fold. He has threatened me and the child with measureless evil if I say this or that against anything he does.' And as every one knows, when Nicol is angry the earth itself turns inside out before him."

"I do not fear him a jot–not I!"

"If you had ever seen him swaggering and rolling from one day into another, if you had ever seen him stroking his bare arms and peering round with wicked eyes for some one to ease him of his temper, you would not say such words."

"I will not call my words back for much more than that, and I will follow up this quarrel."

"If you are foolish, you may do so; if you are wise, you will be neither for nor against Nicol Sinclair. There is a wide and a safe way between these two. Let me tell you, Nanna's life lies in it. I have not yet told you all."

"Speak the last word, then."

"Think what cruel things a bad man can always do to a good woman; all of them Nicol Sinclair has done to your cousin Nanna. Yes, it is so. When she was too weak to hold her baby in her arms he bade her 'die, and make way for a better woman.' And one night he lured her to the cliff-top, and then and there he quarreled with her; and men think—yes, and women think so too—that he threw the child into the water, and that Nanna leaped after it. That was the story in every one's mouth."

"Was it true? Tell me that."

"There was more than guesswork to go on. Magnus Crawford took them out of the sea, and the child was much hurt, for it has never walked, nor yet spoken a word, and there are those who say it never will."

"And what said my cousin Nanna?"

"She held her peace both to men and women; but what she said to God on the matter he knows. It is none of thy business. She has grown stronger and quieter with every sorrow; and it is out of a mother's strength, I tell thee, and not her weakness, that good can come."

Then David rose to his feet and began to walk furiously about the small room. His face was white as death, and he spoke with a still intensity, dropping each word as if it were a separate oath.

"I wish that Sinclair were here—in this room! I would lay his neck across my knee, and break it like a dog's. I would that!"

"It would be a joy to see thee do it. I would say, 'Well done, David Borson!'"

"I am glad that God has made Tophet for such men!" cried David, passionately. "Often I have trembled at the dreadful justice of the Holy One; I see now how good it is. To be sure, when God puts his hook into the nose of the wicked, and he is made to go a way he does not want to go, then he has to cease from troubling. But I wish not that he may cease from being troubled. No, indeed; I wish that he may have weeping and wailing! I will stay here. Some day Sinclair will come back; then he shall pay all he owes."

Suddenly David remembered his father's sad confession, and he was silent. The drowning of Bele Trenby and all that followed it flashed like a fiery thought through his heart, and he went into his room, and shut the door, and flung himself face downward upon the floor. Would God count his anger as very murder? Would he enter into judgment with him for it? Oh, how should a sinful man order all his way and words aright! And in a little while Barbara heard him weeping, and she said to herself:

NANNA AND VALA

"He is a good man. God loves those who remember him when they are alone and weep. The minister said that."

This day had indeed been to David a kind of second birth. He had entered into a new life and taken possession of himself. He knew that he was a different being from the youth who had sailed for weeks alone with God upon the great waters; but still he was a riddle to himself, and it was this feeling of utter confusion and weakness and ignorance that had sent him, weeping and speechless, to the very feet of the divine Father.

But if the mind is left quite passive we are often instructed in our sleep. David awakened with a plan of life clearly in his mind. He resolved to remain with Barbara Traill, and follow his occupation of fishing, and do all that he could to make his cousin Nanna happy. The intense strength of his family affection led him to this resolve. He had not fallen in love with Nanna. As a wife she was sacred in his eyes, and it never entered his mind that any amount of ill treatment could lessen Sinclair's claim upon her. But though far off, she was his cousin; the blood of the Borsons flowed alike through both their hearts; and David, who could feel for all humanity, could feel most of all for Nanna and Vala.

Nanna herself had acknowledged this claim. He remembered how gladly she had welcomed him; he could feel yet the warm clasp of her hand, and the shining of her eyes was like nothing he had ever before seen. Even little Vala had been pleased to lie in his strong arms. She had put up her small mouth for him to kiss, and had slept an hour upon his breast. As he thought of that kiss he felt it on his lips, warm and sweet. Yes, indeed; there was love in that poor little hut that David Borson could not bear to lose.

So he said to Barbara in the morning: "I will stay with you while it pleases us both."

And Barbara answered: "A great help and comfort thou wilt be to me, and doubtless God sent thee."

VI
KINDRED–THE QUICK AND THE DEAD

Shetland was, then, to be David's home, and he accepted the destiny gladly. He felt near to the people, and he admired the old gray town, with its roving, adventurous population. His first duty was to remove his personal belongings from his boat to Barbara Traill's house, and when this was done it was easy enough to set himself to business; for as soon as he went among the fishers and said, "My name is Borson, and I am the son of your old mate Liot Borson," he found himself in a circle of outstretched hands. And as he had brought his nets and lines with him, he had no difficulty in getting men who were glad to help him with his fishing, and to instruct him in the peculiarities of the coast and the set of its tides and currents.

For the rest, there was no sailor or fisher in Lerwick who was so fearless and so wise in all sea-lore as David Borson. Sink or swim, he was every inch a seaman. He read the sea as a landsman reads a book; he knew all its moods and its deceitfulness, and the more placid it was the more David mistrusted its intentions; he was always watching it. The men of Uig had been wont to say that David Borson would not turn his back on the sea, lest it should get some advantage over him. This intimacy of mistrust was the result of his life's training; it was the practical education of nearly twenty years.

His next move was to see the minister and present to him the letter from the minister of Uig, which authenticated his kirk standing and his moral character. He put on his kirk clothes for this call, and was sorry afterward that he had so hampered himself; for the good man met him with both hands outstretched, and blessed him in the name of the Lord.

"I married your father and mother, David," he said. "I baptized you into the fold of Lerwick kirk, and I buried your sweet mother in its quiet croft. Your father was near to me and dear to me. A good man was Liot Borson— a good man! When that is said, what more is left to say? While my life-days last I shall not forget Liot Borson." And then they talked of David's life in Uig, and when he left the manse he knew that he had found a friend.

It was then Thursday night, and he did not care to go to the fishing until the following Monday. Before he began to serve himself he wished to serve God, and so handsel his six days' work by the blessing of the seventh. This was the minister's advice to him, and he found that every one thought it right and good; so, though he made his boat ready for sea, she was not to try her speed and luck on her new fishing-ground until David had offered up thanksgiving for his safe journey, and supplications for grace and wisdom to guide his new life aright.

"There is no more that I can do now until the early tide on Monday morning," he said to Barbara Traill, "and I will see if I can find any more of my kin-folk. Are any of my mother's family yet living?"

"The Sabistons have all gone south to the Orkneys. They are handy at money-getting, and the rumor goes abroad that they are rich and masterful, and ill to deal with; but they were ever all that, or the old tellings-up do them much wrong."

"Few people are better spoken of than they deserve."

"That is so. Yet no one in Lerwick is so well hated as your great-aunt Matilda Sabiston. She is the last of the family left in Shetland. Go and see her if you wish to; I have nothing to say against it; but I can give you a piece of advice: lean not for anything on Matilda Sabiston."

"All I want of her is a little love for my mother's sake; so I will go and see her. For the sake of the dead she will at least be civil."

"Nothing will come of the visit. It is not to be expected that Matilda will behave well to you, when she behaves ill to every one else."

"For all that, I would like to look upon her. We are blood-kin. I have a right to see her face; I have a right to offer her my service and my duty; whether she will take it or throw it from her is to be seen."

"She will *not* take it. However, here is your dinner ready, and after you have eaten it go and see your kinswoman. You will easily find her; she lives in the largest house in Lerwick."

The little opposition to his desires confirmed David in his resolve. When he had eaten, and dressed himself in his best clothing, he went to Matilda Sabiston's house. It was a large stone dwelling, and had been famous for the unusual splendor of its furnishing. David was astonished and interested, but not in the least abashed; for the absorbing idea in his mind was that of kindred, and the soft carpets, the velvet-covered chairs and sofas, the pictures and ornaments, were only the accessories of the condition. An old woman, grim and of few words, opened the heavy door, and then tottered slowly along a narrow flagged passage before him until they came to a somberly furnished parlor, where Mistress Sabiston was sitting, apparently asleep.

"Wake up, mistress," said the woman. "Here be some one that wants to see you."

"A beggar, then, either for kirk or town. I have nothing to give."

"Not so; he is a fair, strong lad, who says you are his aunt."

"He lies, whoever he is. Let me see the fool, Anita."

"Here he is, mistress. Let him speak for himself." And Anita stood aside and permitted David to enter the room.

Matilda sat in a large, uncushioned chair of black wood—the chair of her fore-elder Olaf, who had made it in Iceland from some rare drift, and brought it with his other household goods to Shetland ten generations past. It was a great deal too large for her shrunken form, and her old, old face against its blackness looked as if it had been carved out of the yellow ivory of Sudan. Never had David seen a countenance so void of expression; it was like a scroll made unreadable by the wear and dust of years. Life appeared to have retreated entirely to her eyes, which were fierce and darkly glowing. And the weight and coldness of her great age communicated itself; he was chilled by her simple presence.

"What is your business?" she asked.

"I am the son of your niece Karen."

"I have no niece."

"Yea, but you have. Death breaks no kinship. It is souls that are related, not bodies; and souls live forever."

"Babble! In a word, what brought you here?"

"I came only to see you."

"Well, then, I sent not for you."

"Yet I thought you would wish to see me."

"I do not."

"Liot Borson is dead."

"I am glad of it. He was a murderer while he lived, and now I hope that he is a soul in pain forevermore."

"I am his son, and you must not—"

"Then what brought you here? I have hoped you were dead for many a year. If all the Borsons, root and branch, were gone to their father the devil, it would be a pleasure to me. I have ever hated them; to all who knew them they were bringers of bad luck," she muttered angrily, looking into David's face with eyes full of baleful fire.

"Yet is love stronger than hate, and because my mother was of your blood and kin I will not hate you."

"Hear a wonder!" she screamed. "The man will not hate me. Son of a murderer, I want not one kind thought from you."

"There is no cause to call my father what neither God nor man has called him."

"Cause enough! I know that right well."

"Then it is only right you give proof of such assertions. Say what you mean and be done with it."

"Ah! you are getting angry at last. Your father would have been spitting fire before this. But it was not with fire he slew Bele Trenby–no, indeed; it was with water. Did he not tell you so when he stood on the brink of Tophet?"

"God did not suffer his soul to be led near the awful place. When he gave up his ghost he gave it up to the merciful Father of spirits. It is wicked to speak lies of the living; it is abominable and dangerous to speak ill of the dead."

"I fear neither the living nor the dead. I will say to my last breath that Liot Borson murdered Bele Trenby. He was long minded to do the deed; at last he did it."

"How can you alone, of all the men and women in Lerwick, know this?"

"That night I dreamed a dream. I saw the moss and the black water, and Bele's white, handsome face go down into it. And I saw your father there. What for? That he might do the murder in his heart."

"The dream came from your own thoughts."

"It came from Bele's angel. The next day–yes, and many times afterward–I took to the spot the dog that loved Bele, and the creature whined and crouched to his specter. Men are poor, sightless creatures; animals see spirits where we are blind as bats."

"Are these your proofs? Why do people suffer you to say such things?"

"Because in their hearts they believe me. Murders tell tales; secretly, in the night, crossing the moss, when men are not thinking, they breathe suspicion; they speak after being long dumb. Fifty years is not the date of their bond. They haunt the place of their tragedy, and men dream of the deed. So it is. The report sticks to Liot, and more will come of it yet. Oh, that he were in your shoes to-day! I would find the strength to slay him, if I died and went to hell for it."

"Woman, why dost thou damn thyself while yet there is a hope of mercy?"

"Mercy! What have you to do with mercy? One thing rejoices me: it will not be long ere I meet that blessed thrall that cursed all the generations of the Borsons. He and I will strike hands in that quarrel; and it shall go ill with you and your children till the last Borson be cursed off the face of the earth."

"I will flee unto the Omnipotent. He will keep even my shadow from the evil ones that follow after. Now I will go, for I see there is no hope of good-will between us two."

"And it is my advice that you go away from Shetland."

"That I will *not* do. There are my cousins Nanna and Vala here; and it is freely said that you have done them much ill. I will stay here and do them all the good I can."

"Then you will have Nicol Sinclair to settle with. That is the best of my wish. Nicol Sinclair is my third cousin, and I have given him five hundred pounds because he hates the Borsons and is ready to cross their happiness in all things possible. Pack, now, from my presence! I have no more to say to you. I am no kin to you, and I have taken good care to prevent the law making you kin. My will is made. All that I have not given to Nicol Sinclair goes to make free the slaves in Africa. Freedom! freedom! freedom!" she shrieked. "Nothing is cruel but slavery."

It was the old Norse passion for liberty, strong and vital when every other love was ashes. It was a passion also to which David instantly responded. The slumbering sentiment awoke like a giant in his heart, and he comprehended it by a racial instinct as passionate as her own.

"You have done well," he said. "Hunger and cold, pain and poverty, are nothing if one has freedom. It is a grand thing to set a man or a woman *free.*"

"And yet you catch haddock and herring! Bah! we have nothing to do with each other."

"Then farewell, aunt, and God give you mercy in the day you will need mercy."

She was suddenly and stolidly silent. She fixed her eyes on the dull glow of the burning peats, and relapsed into the torpor that was her habitual mood. Its force was insurmountable. David went slowly out of her presence, and was unable for some time to cast off the depression of her icy influence. Yet the meeting had not been without result. During it he had felt the first conscious throb of that new passion for freedom which had sprung into existence at the impetuous, glowing iteration of the mere word from his aunt's lips. He felt its charm in the unaccustomed liberty of his own actions. He was now entirely without claims but those his love or liking voluntarily assumed. No one older than himself had the right to reprove or direct him. He had at last come to his majority. He was master of himself and his fate.

The first evidence of this new condition was a dignified reticence with Barbara Traill. She was conscious of the change in her lodger. She felt instinctively that he was no longer a child to be questioned, and there was a tone of authority in his refusal to discuss his aunt Sabiston with her which she could not but respect. Indeed, it was no longer possible to speak to him of Mistress Sabiston as Mistress Sabiston deserved to be spoken of. Her first censure was checked by David's air of disapproval and his few words of apology:

"She is, however, my aunt; and when one is ninety years old it is a good excuse for many faults."

Matilda's utter refusal of his kin or kindness threw him more exclusively upon Nanna and her child. And as all his efforts to discover any other family connections were quite futile, he finally came to believe that they three were the last of a family that had once filled the lands of the Norsemen with the fame of their great deeds. Insensibly this thought drew the bond tighter and closer, though an instinct as pure as it was conventional taught him a scrupulous delicacy with regard to this friendship. Fortunately, in Shetland the blood-tie was regarded as a strong enough motive for all David's attentions to a woman and child so desolate and helpless. People said simply, "It is a good thing for Nanna Sinclair that her cousin has come to Shetland." And it did not enter their hearts to imagine an evil motive for kind deeds when there was one so natural and obligatory.

So Shetland became dear and pleasant to David, and he gradually grew into great favor. The minister made much of the young man, for he respected his integrity and earnest piety, and loved him for that tenderness and clearness of conscience which was sensitive to the first approaches of wrong. The fishers and sailors of the town gave him a warm admiration for his seamanship, and the praise David had looked for at the beginning, and felt disappointed in not receiving, was now given him by a kind of acclamation. Old sailors, telling yarns of their ships and the queer, bold things their ships had done, generally in some way climaxed their narratives by an allusion to David Borson. Thus, Peter Redlands, talking to a group of fishers one day, said:

"Where that lad learned the sea, and who taught him all the ways of it, is beyond me; but say as you will, he can make harbor when none of us could look at it. It is my belief David Borson can stick to anything that can float."

"And to see how he humors a boat," continued Jan Wyck, "you would think she was made out of flesh instead of out of three-inch planks. I was out with him near the Old Man's Rocks last week, and he was watching the water; and I said, 'What is it, David?' 'The sea,' he said. 'It will be at its old tricks again in an hour or less.' And the 'less' was right, for in fifteen minutes the word was, 'Reef, and quick about it!' and then you know what— the rip and the roar, and the boat leaping her full length. But David did not worry a jot. He coaxed her beautifully, and kept her well in hand; and she shook herself a little, and then away like a gull before the wind."

He was just as popular among the children and women of Lerwick. The boys made an idol of him, for David was always ready to give them a sail, or lend them his fowling-piece, or help them to rig their toy boats. As for the maidens, the prettiest ones in Lerwick had a shy smile for David Borson, and many wondered that such a beauty as Asta Fae should smile on him in vain; but David had taken Nanna and Vala into his heart, and his care and thought for them were so constant that there was no room for any other interest. Yet Barbara often talked to him about taking a wife; and even the minister, doubtless led to such advice by female gossip and speculation, thought it well to speak a word on the subject to him.

"You know, David," he said, "there are good girls and beautiful girls that look kindly on you, and who wonder that your smiles are so cold and your words so few; and it is my duty to say to you that evil may come of your taking so much thought for your cousin and her child, and the way to help her best is to help her through your own wife."

"I am not in the mind to marry, minister," he answered. "There is no one girl dearer or fairer to me than another. And as for what I do for my cousins, I think that God sent me to do it, and I shall not be feared to make accounting to him for it."

"That is my belief also, David. Yet we are told to avoid the very appearance of evil; and what is more, if it is not your pleasure to marry, it is your duty; and how will you win past that?"

"I have not seen it to be my duty, minister."

"The promise is in the line of the righteous; the blessing is for you and for your children; but if you have no wife or children, then is the promise shortened and the blessing cut off. I think that you should choose some good woman's daughter, and build yourself a home, and then marry a wife."

The young man went out of the manse with this thought in his heart. And not far off he met pretty Asta Fae, and he spoke to her and walked with her as far as she was going; and he saw that she had the sweetest of blue eyes, and that her smile was tender and her ways gentle. And when he left her at her father's door, he held her hand a moment and said, "It has been a pleasant walk to me, Asta." And she looked frankly into his face and answered with rosy blushes, "And to me also, David."

There was a warm glow at his heart as he went across the moor to Nanna's; and he resolved to tell his cousin what the minister had said, and ask her advice about Asta Fae; but when he reached Nanna's cot she was sitting on the hearth with Vala upon her knees, and telling her such a strange story that David would not for anything lose a word of it. And as Nanna's back was to the open door she did not see David enter, but went on with her tale, in the high, monotonous tone of one telling a narrative whose every word is well known and not to be changed.

"You see, Vala," she said, touching the child's fingers and toes, "it was the old brown bull of Norraway, and he had a sore battle with the deil, and he carried off a great princess; and you may know how big he was, for he said to her, 'Eat out of my left ear, and drink out of my right ear, and put by the leavings.' And ay they rode, and on they rode, till they came to a dark and awesome glen, and there the bull stopped and the lady lighted down. And the bull said to her: 'Here you must stay while I go on and fight the deil. And you must sit here on that stone, and move not hand or foot till I come back, or else I'll never find you again. And if everything round about you turns blue, I shall have beaten the deil; but if all things turn red, then the deil will have conquered me.'"

"And so he left her, mammy, to go and fight the deil?"

"Ay, he did, Vala; and she sat still, singing."

"Sing me the lady's song, mammy."

Then Nanna intoned softly the strangest, wildest little tune. It was like a Gregorian chant, and had but three notes, but to these she gave a marvelous variety. David listened spellbound to the entreating voice:

"'Seven long years I served for thee,

The glassy hill I clamb for thee,

The bloody shirt I wrang for thee,

And wilt thou not waken and come to me?'

But I'm thinking he never came back to the lady."

"Oh, yes, he did, mammy," said Vala, confidently. "Helga Storr told me he came back a fine prince with a gold crown on his head, and the deil went away empty and roaring mad."

"What is it you are telling about, Nanna?" said David, his face eager and alight with interest.

She rose up then, with Vala in her arms, her eyes shining with her sweet, motherly story-telling. "It is only an old tale, David," she answered. "I know not who made it up. My mother told it to me, and her mother to her, and so back through years that none can count. Yes, indeed; what little child does not know the story of the big brown bull of Norraway?"

"I never heard of it before," said David.

"To be sure; your mother did not live to talk to you—poor little lad!"

"Now, then, Nanna, tell it to me for my mother's sake." And he sat down on the cricket by her side, and took Vala on his knee; and Nanna laughed, and then, with the little formal importance of the reciter, said: "Well, so it shall be, then. Here beginneth the story of the big brown bull of Norraway and his fight with the deil." And the old tale fell from her lips full of charm, and David listened with all the delight of a child. And when it had been twice told, Nanna began to talk of the burnt Njal and the Icelandic sagas, and the more so as she saw David was full of strange wonder and delight, and that every word was fresh and enthralling to him.

"Yet it is a thing to be wondered at," she said finally, "that you, David, know not these old histories better than I do; for I have often heard that no one in all the islands could tell a story so well as Liot Borson. Yes, and the minister once said, and I heard him, that he would walk ten miles to hear from your father's lips once more the sad happenings of his ancestor, the brave, helpful Gisli."

"This is a great thing to me, Nanna," answered David, in a voice low and quiet, for he was feeling deeply. "And I look to you now for what has never been told me. Who, then, was my ancestor Gisli?"

"If your father held his peace about him, he surely thought it best to do so, and so ask me not to break a good resolve."

"Nay, but I must ask you. My heart burns; I feel that there is a life behind me into which I must look. Help me, Nanna. And, more, the name Gisli went to my head. It is not like other strange names. I love this man whom I have not seen and never heard of until this hour. What has he to do with me?"

"*He was one of us.* And because he was so good and great the thrall's curse fell the harder on him, and was the more regarded—hard enough it has been on all the Borsons; and perhaps your father thought it was well you heard not of it. Many a time and oft I have wished it had not entered my ears; for when one sorrow called to another sorrow, and one wrong trod on the heels of another wrong, I have been angry at the false, ungrateful man who brought such ill fortune upon his unborn generations."

"Now you make me so anxious and wilful that nothing but the story of the thrall's curse will do for me. I shall not eat or sleep till I hear it."

"'Tis a tale of dishonor and unthankfulness, and not so well known to me as to Jorn Thorkel. He can tell it all, and will gladly do so."

"But for all that, I will hear it from you, Nanna, and you only, for it concerns us only. Tell me what you know, and the rest can wait for Jorn."

"So, then, you will have it; but if ill comes of the knowledge do not blame me. It began in the days of Harold Fairhair, one thousand years ago. There was a Gisli then, and he had a quarrel with a berserker called Bjorn, and they agreed to fight until one was dead. And the woman who loved Gisli told him that her foster-father, Kol, who was a thrall, had a sword that whoever wielded would win in any fight. And Gisli sent for Kol and asked him:

"'Hast thou ever a good sword?'

"And Kol answered: 'Many things are in the thrall's cot, not in the king's grange.'

"'Lend me thy sword for my duel with Bjorn,' said Gisli.

"And Kol said: 'Then this thing will happen: thou wilt never wish to give it up. And yet I tell thee, this sword will bite whatever it falls on, nor can its edge be deadened by spells, for it was forged by the dwarfs, and its name is Graysteel. And make up thy mind,' he said, 'that I will take it very ill indeed if I get not my sword back when I ask for it.'

"So Gisli took the sword and slew Bjorn with it, and got good fame for this feat. And time rolled on, and he gave not back the sword; and one day Kol met him, and Gisli had Graysteel in his hand, and Kol had an ax.

"And Kol asked if the sword had done him good service at his great need, and Gisli was full of its praises.

"'Well, now,' said Kol, 'I should like it back.'

"'Sell it to me,' said Gisli.

"'No,' said Kol.

"'I will give thee thy freedom for it,' said Gisli.

"'I will not sell it,' said Kol.

"'I will also give thee land and sheep and cattle and goods as much as thou wantest,' said Gisli.

"'I will not sell it a whit more for that,' said Kol.

"'Put thy own price on it in money, and I will get thee a fair wife also,' said Gisli.

"'There is no use talking about it,' said Kol. 'I will not sell it, whatsoever thou offerest. It has come to what I said would happen: that thou wouldst not give me back my weapon when thou knewest what virtue was in it.'

"'And I too will say what will happen,' said Gisli. 'Good will befall neither of us; for I will *not* give up the sword, and it shall never come into any man's hand but mine, if I have my will.'

"Then Kol lifted his ax, and Gisli drew Graysteel, and they smote at each other. Kol's blow fell on Gisli's head, so that it sank into the brain; and Graysteel fell on Kol's head, and his skull was shattered, and Graysteel broke asunder. Then, as Kol gave up the ghost, he said:

"'It had been better that thou hadst given me my sword when I asked for it, for this is only the beginning of the ill fortune I will bring on thy kith and kin forever.'

"And so it has been. For a thousand years the tellings-up of our family are full of troubles that this thrall's curse has brought upon us. Few of our men have grown gray-headed; in the sea and on the battlefield they have found their graves; and the women have had sorrow in marriage and death in child-bearing."

"It was an evil deed," said David.

"It was a great curse for it also; one thousand years it has followed Gisli's children."

"Not so! I believe it not! Neither the dead nor the living can curse those whom God blesses."

"Yet always the Borsons have had the worst of ill fortune. We three only are now left of the great earls who ruled in Surnadale and in Fjardarfolk, and see how poor and sorrowful we are. My life has been woven out of grief and disappointment; Vala will never walk; and as for your own youth, was it not labor and sorrow only?"

"I believe not in any such spaedom. I believe in God the Father Almighty, and in Jesus Christ, and in the Holy Ghost. And as for the cursing of man, dead or alive, I will not fear what it can do to me. Gisli was indeed well served for his mean, ungrateful deed, and it would have been better if the berserker Bjorn had cut his false heart out of him."

"Such talk is not like you, David. I can see now that your father did right to keep these bloody stories from your hearing. There is no help in them."

"Well, I know not that. This night the minister was talking to me about taking a wife. If there be truth or power in Kol's curse, why should any Borson be born, that he or she may bear his spite? No; I will not marry, and–"

"In saying that you mock your own words. Where, then, is your trust in God? And the minister is right; you ought to take a wife. People think wrong of a young man who cannot fix his heart on one good woman. There is Christina Hey. Speak to her. Christina is sweet and wise, and will make a good wife."

"I met Asta Fae as I came here. Very pretty indeed is her face, and she has a way to win any heart."

"For all that, I do not think well of Asta. She is at the dance whenever there is one, and she has more lovers than a girl should have."

"Christina has land and money. I care not for a wife who is richer than myself."

"Her money is nothing against her; it will be a help."

"I know not," he answered, but without interest. "You have given me something to think of that is better than wooing and wedding, Nanna. My heart is quite full. I am more of a man than I have ever been. I can feel this hour that there is life behind me as well as before me. But I will go now, for to-morrow is the Sabbath and we shall meet at the kirk; and I will carry Vala home for you if you say so, Nanna."

"Well, then," she answered, "to-morrow is not here, David; but it will come, by God's leave. I dreamed a dream last night, and I look for a change, cousin. But this or that, my desire is that God would choose for me."

"That also is my desire," said David, solemnly.

"As for me, I have fallen into a great strait; only God can help me."

She was standing on the hearth, looking down at Vala. Tears were in her eyes, and a divine pity and sorrow made tender and gentle her majestic beauty. David looked steadily at her, and something, he knew not what, seemed to pierce his very soul–a sweet, aching pain, never felt before, inexplicable, ineffable, and as innocent as the first holy adoration of a little child. Then he went out into the still, starry night, and tried to think of Christina Hey; but she constantly slipped from his consciousness, like a dream that has no message.

VII
SO FAR AND NO FARTHER

David Borson was stirred to the very seat of life by the things Nanna had told him. It did not enter his heart to doubt their truth. The shameful deed of the first Gisli, and the still strong order of its consequences, which neither the guilt of his children hastened, nor their innocence delayed, nor their expiation arrested, was the dominant feeling aroused by her narrative. The whole story, with its terrible Nemesis, fitted admirably into the system of Calvinistic theology, and David had not yet come to the hour in which faith would crush down fatalism. The words of these ancient sagas went singing and swinging through his brain and heart, and life seemed so wonderful and bewildering, its sorrows so great and certain, its needs so urgent and present, and heaven, alas! so far off.

There came to him also, as he slowly trod the lonely moor, the most awful of all conceptions of eternity—the revelation of *a repentance that could undo nothing*. He was righteously angry at Gisli's base ingratitude; he was sorry for his sin; but others had doubtless felt the same anger and sorrow, and it had been ineffectual. Helpless and passive in the hands of destiny, a nameless dread, an urgent want of help and comfort, forced him to feel out into the abyss for something more than flesh and blood to lean on; and then he found that God is best of all approached in indefinite awe and worship, and that moments of tender, vague mystery, haunted by uncertain presentiments, bring him near.

"Well, then," he said as he came to the door of his house, "the wicked may be a rod, and smite for generations; but the rod is in the hand of God, and I will remind myself that my God is the Everlasting, Almighty, Infinite One; and I will ask him to give sentence with me, and to deliver me from the wicked, whether they be in the body or out of the body." And he walked through the house-place where Barbara was sitting, and saw her not; for he was saying to himself, "'Why art thou so vexed, O my soul? and why art thou disquieted within me? O put thy trust in God: for I will yet give him thanks, which is the help of my countenance, and my God.'"

Nanna sat motionless for long after David left her. She had many causes for anxiety. She was fearful of losing her work, and absolute poverty would then be her lot. It was a fear, however, and not a certainty; and after a little reflection she also threw her care upon the Preserver of men. "Be at peace," she said to her heart. "God feeds the gulls and the ravens, and he will not starve Nanna and Vala."

It was harder to combat her spiritual anxieties. She was sorry she had told David about the thrall's curse. Her first instinct was to ask his father and mother to forgive her; then she suddenly remembered that praying to or for the dead was a sin for a kirk session to meet on. And this thought led her easily to the dream that had troubled her last night's sleep and made her day dark with sorrowful fears. All her life she had possessed something of that sixth sense by which we see and anticipate things invisible. And it is noticeable that many cripples have often a seraphic intelligence, a far-reaching vision, and very sensitive spiritual aptitudes. Vala was of this order. She too had been singularly depressed; she had seen more than she could tell; she was as restless and melancholy as birds just before their migrations, and she looked at her mother with eyes so wistful, so full of inquiry, so "far off," that Nanna trembled under their fearfully prescient intimations. Alas for the dangerous happiness of maternity! How prodigious are its inquietudes! How uncertain its consolations!

She told David that she had dreamed a dream, and that she looked for a change; and she had made this statement as simply and as confidently as if she had said, "The wind is from the north, and I look for a storm." Repeated experiences had taught her, as they teach constantly, that certain signs precede certain events, and that certain dreams are dictated by that delicate antenna of spiritual instinct which feels danger to be near and warns of it.

Nanna had had *the dream* that ever forecast her misfortunes, and she sat thinking of its vague intimations, and tightening her heart for any sorrow. She had been forewarned that she might be forearmed, and she regarded this warning as a mark of interest and favor from beyond the veil. God had always spoken to his children in dreams and by the oracles that abide in darkness, and Nanna knew that in many ways "dreams are large possessions." She fell asleep pondering what her vision of the preceding night might mean, and awoke next morning, while it was still dark, with a dim sense of fear and sorrow encompassing her.

"But everything frightens one when night, the unknown, takes the light away," she thought. And she rose and lighted a lamp, and looked at Vala. The child was in a deep and healthy slumber, and the sight of its face calmed and satisfied her. Yet she was strangely apprehensive, and there was a weight on her heart that made her faint and trembling. She knew right well that some hitherto unknown sorrow was creeping like a mist over her life, and she had not yet the strength and the pang of conflict.

Have we not too? Yes, we have

   Answers, and we know not whence;

Echoes from beyond the grave,

   Recognized intelligence.

Yet the secret silence of the night, the vague terror and darkness of that occult world which we all carry with us, created in her, at first, fear, and then a kind of angry, desperate resentment.

"Oh, how helpless I am!" she sighed. "I can think and feel, I can fear and love, and I am not here by my own will; I did not place myself here; I cannot keep myself here. My life is in the grasp of a Power I cannot control. What am I to do? What can I do? Oh, how miserable I am! All my life long I have seen '*Not for you*' written on all I wished. Life is very hard," she said with a little sob. And then she made no further complaint, but her heart grew so still, she was sure something must have died there. Alas! was it hope?

"Life is very hard." With these words she lay down again, and between sleeping and waking the hours wore on, and she rose at last from her shivery sleep, even later than usual. Then she hurried breakfast a little, and as the light grew over land and sea she tidied her room and dressed Vala and herself for the kirk. As the sound of the first service bell traveled solemnly over the moor she was ready to leave the house. Her last duty was to put a peat or two upon the fire, and as she was doing this she heard some one lift the sneck and push open the door.

"It is David to carry Vala," she thought. "How good he is!"

But when she turned she saw that it was not David. It was her husband, Nicol Sinclair. He walked straight to the fireside, and sat down without a word. Nanna's heart sank to its lowest depths, and a cold despair made her feet and hands heavy as lead; but she slowly spread the cloth on the table, and bit by bit managed to recollect the cup and saucer, the barley-cake, the smoked goose, and the tea.

There was a terrible account between the man sitting on the hearth and herself, and words of passionate reproach burned at her lips; but she held her peace. Long ago she had left her cause with God; he would plead it thoroughly. Even now, when her enemy was before her, she had no thought of any other advocate.

Her pallor, her slow movements, her absolute dumbness, roused in Sinclair an angry discomfort. And when Vala made a movement he lifted her roughly, and with a brutal laugh said, "A nice plaything you will be on board the *Sea Rover*!"

Nanna shivered at the words. She comprehended in a moment the torture this man had probably come purposely to inflict upon her. Already his cruel hands had crippled her child; and what neglect, what terrors, what active barbarities, might he not impose on the little one in the hell of his own ship! Who there could prevent him? Little did Nicol Sinclair care for public opinion on land; but out at sea, where Vala's tears and cries could bring her no help, what pitiless inhumanities might he not practise?

"*Fly with the child!*"

The words were struck upon her heart like blows. But how should she fly? and where to? Far or near, the law would find her out and would give Vala to her father's authority. And she had no friend strong enough to protect her. Only by death could she defy separation. Thus, while she was pouring the boiling water on the tea-leaves, she was revolving questions more agonizing than words have power to picture.

At length the food was on the table, and, save for those few threatening words, the silence was unbroken. Sinclair sat down to his meal with a bravado very near to cursing, and at that moment the kirk bells began to ring again. To Nanna they were like a voice from heaven. Quick as thought she lifted her child and fled from the house.

"BUT SHE HELD HER PEACE."

Oh, what stress of life and death was in her footsteps! Only to reach the kirk! If she could do that, she would cling to the altar and die there rather than surrender Vala to unknown miseries. Love and terror gave her wings. She did not turn her head; she did not feel the frozen earth or the cutting east wind; she saw nothing but Vala's small face on her breast, and she heard nothing but the echo in her heart of those terrible words threatening her with the loss of her child.

When she reached the kirk the service had begun. The minister was praying. She went into the nearest pew, and though all were standing, she laid Vala on the seat, and slipped to her knees beside her. She could not now cry out as she longed to do, and sob her fright and anguish away at God's feet. "Folk would wonder at me. I would disturb the service." These were her thoughts as soon as the pressure of her flight was over. For the solemn voice of the minister praying, the strength of numbers, the holy influence of the time and place, cooled her passionate sense of wrong and danger, and she was even a little troubled at her abandonment of what was usual and Sabbath-like.

The altar now looked a long way off; only Sinclair at touch could have forced her down that guarded aisle to its shelter. Heaven itself was nearer, and God needed no explanations. He knew all. What was the law of man to him? And he feared not their disapproval. Thus in her great strait she overleaped her creed, and cast herself on him who is "a God of the afflicted, an helper of the oppressed, an upholder of the weak, a protector of the forlorn, a savior of them that are without hope."

When the preaching was over David and Barbara came to her; and David knit his brows when he saw her face, for it was the face of a woman who had seen something dreadful. Her eyes were full of fear and anguish, and she was yet white and trembling with the exertion of her hard flight.

"Nanna," he said, "what has happened?"

"My husband has come back."

"I heard last night that his ship was in harbor."

"He has come for Vala. He will take her from me. She will die of neglect and hard usage. He may give her to some stranger who will be cross to her. O David! David!"

"He shall not touch her."

"O David!"

"Put her in my arms *now*."

"Do you mean this?"

"I do."

"Can I trust you, David?"

"You may put it to any proof."

"Pass your word to me, cousin."

"As the Lord God Almighty lives, I will put my life between Vala and Nicol Sinclair!"

"But how?"

"I will take her to sea if necessary, for my boat can go where few will dare to follow."

Then he turned to Barbara and said: "Nicol Sinclair has indeed come back. He says he has come for Vala."

AT THE KIRK.

"Then the devil has led him here," answered Barbara, flashing into anger. "As for Vala, let her stay with me. She has a good guard at my house. There is Groat and his four sons on one side, and Jeppe Madson and his big brother Har on the other side; and there is David Borson, who is worth a whole ship's crew, to back them in anything for Vala's safety. Stay with me to-day, Nanna, and we will talk this matter out."

But Nanna shook her head in reply. As she understood it, duty was no peradventure; it was an absolute thing from which there was no turning away. And her duty was to be at home when her husband was there. But she put Vala's hand into David's hand, and then looked at the young man with eyes full of anxiety. He answered the look with one strong word:

"*Yes!*"

And she knew he would redeem it with his life, if that should be necessary.

Then she turned homeward, and walked with a direct and rapid energy. She put away thought; she formed no plan, she said no prayer. Her petition had been made in the kirk; she thought there would be a want of faith in repeating a request already promised. She felt even the modesty of a suppliant, and would not continually press into the presence of the Highest; for to the reverent there is ever the veil before the Shechinah.

And this conscious putting aside of all emotion strengthened her. When she saw her home she had no need to slacken her speed or to encourage herself. She walked directly to the door and opened it. There was no one there; the place was empty. The food on the table was untouched. Nothing but a soiled and crumpled handkerchief remained of the dreadful visitor. She lifted it with the tongs and cast it into the fire. Then she cleared away every trace of the rejected meal.

Afterward she made some inquiries in the adjoining huts. One woman only had seen his departure. "I could not go to kirk this morning," she said with an air of apology, "for my bairn is very sick; and I saw Nicol Sinclair go away. It was near the noon hour. Drunk he was, and worse drunk than most men can be. His face was red as a hot peat, and he swayed to and fro like a boat on the Gruting Voe. There was something no' just right about the man."

That was all she could learn, and she was very unhappy, for she could imagine no good reason for his departure. In some way or other he was preparing the blow he meant to deal her; and though it was the Sabbath, there would be no difficulty in finding men whom he could influence. And there was also his cousin Matilda Sabiston, that wicked old woman who had outlived all human passions but hatred. Against this man and the money and ill-will that would back him she could do nothing, but she "trusted in God that he would deliver her."

So she said to herself, "Patience"; and she sat down to wait, shutting her eyes to the outside world, and drawing to a focus all the strength that was in her. The closed Bible lay on the table beside her, and occasionally she touched it with her hand. She had not been able to read it; but there was comfort in seeing the old, homely-looking book, with its everyday aspect and its pages full of kindly blessing, and still more comfort in putting herself in physical contact with its promises. They seemed to be more real. And as she sat hour after hour, psalms learned years before, and read many and many a time without apprehension of their meaning, began to speak to her. She saw the words with her spiritual sight, and they shone with their own glory. And she obtained what she so sorely needed:

A little comforting shadow

  From the hot sun's fiery glow;

A little rest by the fountain

  Where the waters of comfort flow.

When midnight struck she looked at the clock and thanked God. Surely she was safe for that night; and she turned the key in her door and went to sleep. And her sleep was that which God giveth to his beloved when they are to be strengthened for many days—a deep, dreamless suspense of all thought and feeling.

Yet, heavenly as the sleep had been, the awakening was a shock. And as the day grew toward noon she was as much troubled by the silence of events as her husband had been by the silence of her lips. Human hearts are nests of fear. Her whole soul kept going to the window, and she said, with the impatience of suspended suffering, "*Now! now!* I have no fortitude for to-morrow, but I can bear anything *now*." Finally she resolved to go to Barbara's, and see Vala, and hear whatever there was to hear. But as she was putting on her cloak she saw David coming over the moor, and he was carrying Vala in his arms.

"So," she said, "I see that I will not need to run after my fate; it will come to me; and there will be no use striving against it. For what must be is sure to happen."

Then she turned back into the house, and David followed with unusual solemnity, and laid Vala upon her bed. "She is sleeping," he said, "and there is something to tell you, Nanna."

"About my husband?"

"Yes."

"Say it out at once, then."

"Last night he was carried to his own ship." And David's face was grave almost to sternness.

"Carried! Have you then hurt him, David?"

"No; he is a self-hurter. But this is what I know. He went from here to Matilda Sabiston's house. She had gone to kirk with two of her servants, and when she came back she found him delirious on the sofa. Then the doctor was sent for, and when he said the word 'typhus,' Matilda shrieked with passion, and demanded that he should be instantly taken away."

"But no! Surely not!"

"Yes; it was so. Both the minister and the doctor said it was right and best for him to be taken to his own ship. The town—yes, indeed, and the whole islands were in danger. And when they took him on board the *Sea Rover*, they found that two of the sailors were also very ill with the fever. They had been ill for a week, and Sinclair knew it; yet he came among the boats, and went through the town, speaking to many people. It was a wicked thing for him to do."

"It was just like him. Where is the *Sea Rover* now lying?"

"She has been taken to the South Voe. The fishing-boats will watch lest the men are landed, and the doctor will go to the ship every day the sea will let him go."

"David, is it my duty—"

"No, it is not; there are five men with Sinclair. Three of them are, I believe, yet well men, and three can care for the sick and the ship. On the deck of the *Sea Rover* a woman should not put her foot."

"But a ship with typhus on board?"

"Is a hell indeed! In this case, Nanna, it is a hell of their own making. They got the fever in a dance-house at Rotterdam. Sinclair knew of its presence, and laughed it to scorn. It was his mate who told the doctor so. Also, Nanna, there is Vala."

She went swiftly to the side of the sleeping child, and she was sure there was a change in her. David would not acknowledge it, but in forty-eight hours the signs of the fatal scourge were unmistakable. Then Nanna's house was marked and isolated, and she sat down to watch her dying child.

VIII
THE JUSTIFICATION OF DEATH

During the awful days of Vala's dying no one came near Nanna. She watched her child night and day, and saw it go out into the darkness that girds our life around, in unutterable desolation of soul. From the first Vala was unconscious, and she went away without a word or token of comfort to the despairing mother. There was unspeakable suffering and decay, and then the little breathing-house in which Vala had sojourned a short space was suddenly vacant. For a moment Nanna stood on the border-lands of being, where life hardly draws breath. *A little more*, and she would have pushed apart the curtains that divide us from that spiritual world which lies so close and which may claim us at any moment. *A little more*, and she would, in her loving agony, have pressed beyond manifestations to that which is ineffable and nameless.

But at the last moment the flesh-and-blood conductor of spirit failed; a great weakness and weariness made her passive under the storm of sorrow that drove like rain to the roots of her life. When she was able to move, Vala lay sad and still. All was over, and Nanna stood astonished, smitten, dismayed, on a threshold she could not pass. The Eternal had given, and it was a gift; he had taken away, and it was an immeasurable loss, and she could not say, "Blessed be the name of the Lord." She was utterly desolate; and when she washed for the last time the little feet that had never trod the moor or street or house, she thought her heart would break. *Who* had led them through the vast spaces of the constellations? *Whither* had they been led? There was no answer to her moaning question. She looked from her dead Vala to God, and all was darkness. She could not see him.

It was a hurried burial in a driving storm. The sea rolled in fateful billows, the winds whistled loud and shrill, the rain soaked Nanna through and through. Two or three of her neighbors followed afar off; they wished her to see they were not oblivious of her grief and loss, but they dared not break the ordinance of town and kirk and voluntarily and without urgent reason come in contact with the contagion; for the island not many years previously had been almost decimated by the same scourge, and every man and woman was the guardian, not only of his or her own life, but of the lives of the community.

Nanna understood this. She saw the dark, cloaked figures of her friends standing in the storm at a distance, and she knew the meaning of their upraised hands; but she had no heart to answer the signal of sympathy.

Alone, she stood by the small open grave and saw it filled. The rain beat on it, and she was glad that it beat on her. It was with difficulty, and only with some affected anger, the two men who had buried the child got her to return to her home.

How vacant it was! How unspeakably lonely! The stormy dreariness outside the cot, the atmosphere of sorrow and loss within it, were depressing beyond words. And what can be said of the loneliness and sorrow within the soul? But in every bitter cup there is one drop bitterest of all; and in Nanna's case this was David's neglect and apparent desertion. She had received no message from him, nor had he come near her in all her trouble. Truly, he must have broken the law to do so; but Nanna was sure no town ordinance would have kept her from David's side in such an hour, and she despised that obedience to law which could teach him such cowardly neglect.

Day after day passed, and he came not. The fever was by this time in all the cottages around her, and the little hamlet was a plague-spot that every one avoided. But, for all that, Nanna's heart condemned her cousin. She tried him by her own feelings, and found him guilty of unpardonable selfishness and neglect. And oh, how dreary are those waste places left by the loved who have deserted us! With what bitter tears we water them! Vala and David had been her last tie to love and happiness. "Thank God," she cried out in her misery, "it can only be broken once!"

Vala had been in her grave a week—a week of days that turned the mother's heart gray—before Nanna heard a word of comfort. Then once more David lifted the latch of the cot and entered her presence. She was sitting still and empty-handed, and her white face and the quivering of her lips pierced him to the heart.

"Nanna! Nanna!" he said.

Then she rose, and looked round the lonely room, and David understood what she meant.

"Nanna! Nanna!" was still all that he could say. He could find no words fit for such sorrow; but there was the truth to speak, and that might have some comfort in it. So he took her hands in his, and said gently:

"Nanna! dear Nanna! your husband is dead."

"I am glad of it!" she answered. "He killed Vala twice over." Her voice was low and weary, and she asked no question about the matter.

"Did you think I had forgotten you, Nanna?"

"Well, then, yes."

"Forgotten you and Vala?"

"It looked most like it. I thought you were either feared for yourself or the law."

"No wonder men think ill of God, whom they do not know, when they are so ready to think ill of men, whom they do know."

"O David! how could you desert me? Can you think of all that I have suffered alone? God nor man has helped me."

"Poor, poor Nanna!"

"If you had been ill to death, neither the words of men nor the power of the law could have kept me from your sick-bed. No, indeed! I would have risked everything to help you. Where were you at all, David?"

"I was on the *Sea Rover*."

"The *Sea Rover*! That is Nicol's ship. What did he do to you? What were you there for?"

"I was on the *Sea Rover* nursing your husband."

"My God!"

"That is the truth, Nanna. I have just finished my task."

"Who sent you?"

"The minister came to me with the order, and I could not win by it and face God and man again."

"What said he? O David! David!"

"He said, 'David Borson, there are four men ill with typhus this morning on the *Sea Rover*. The one man yet unstricken is quite broken down with fright and fatigue. The doctor says some one ought to go there. What do you think?' And I said, 'Minister, do you mean me?' And he smiled a bit and answered, 'I thought you would know your duty, David.'"

"But why *your* duty, David? Surely Vala was dearer and nearer."

"The minister said, 'You are a lone man, David, and you fear God; so, then, you need not fear the fever.'"

"And he knew that you hated Sinclair! Knew that Sinclair had come to my house with the fever on him–knew that he had lifted my poor bairn, only that he might give her the death-kiss!"

"No, no! How could any father, any man, be as bad as that, Nanna?"

"You know not how bad the devil can make a man when he enters into him. And how could the minister send you such a hard road?"

"It was made easy to me; it was indeed, Nanna. The sensible presence of God, and the shining of his face on me, though only for a moment, made me willing to give up all my anger and all my revenge, and wait on my enemy, and do what I could for him to the last moment."

"And Vala? How could you forget her?"

"I did not forget her. I was feared for the child, though I would not say that to you. Barbara told me she had fret all night, and when I said it would be for her mother, the woman shook her head in a way that made me tremble. I was on my way to see her and you when I met the minister, and he sent me the other way."

"Why did you not tell him that you feared for Vala?"

"I said that, and he said, 'Nanna will be able to care for the little one; but there is a strong man needed to care for her husband; Nicol Sinclair will be hard to manage.' And then he minded me of the man's sinful life, and he said peradventure it might be the purpose of God even yet to give him another opportunity for repentance through me."

"If he had known Nicol Sinclair as I—"

"Yes, Nanna, but it is an awful thing to die eternally. If I could help to save any one from such a fate, even my worst enemy,—even your enemy and Vala's,—what should I have done? Tell me."

"Just what you did. You have done right. Yes; though the man killed Vala, you have done right! You have done right!"

"I knew that would be your last word."

"Did he have one good thought, one prayer, to meet death with?"

"He did not. It was a wild night when he was in the dead thraws—a wild night for the flitting; and he went out in storm and darkness, and the sea carried him away."

"God have mercy upon him! I have not a tear left for Nicol Sinclair."

"It was an awful death; but on the same night there was a very good death after a very good life. You have heard, Nanna?"

"I have heard nothing. For many days all has been still and tidingless. The fever is in every house, and no one comes near but the doctor, and he speaks only to the sick."

"Well, then, the good minister has gone home. He was taken with the fever while giving the sacrament to Elder Somerlid. And he knew that he would die, for he said, 'John Somerlid, we shall very soon drink this cup together in the house of our Father in heaven.' So when he got back to the manse he sent for Elder Peterson, and gave him his last words."

"And I know well that they would be good words."

"They were like himself, full of hope. He spoke about his books, and the money in his desk to pay all his debts, and then he said:

"'The days of my life are ended, but I have met the hand of God, Peter, and it is strong to lead and to comfort me. A word was brought to me even as I held the blessed cup in my hand. Read to me from the Book while I can listen to it.' And Peterson asked, 'What shall I read?' And the minister said, 'Take the Psalms. There is everything in the Psalms.' So Peterson read the ones he called for, and after a little the minister said:

"'That will do, Peter. I turn now from the sorrow and pain and darkness of earth to the celestial city, to infinite serenities, to love without limit, to perfect joy. And when I am dead, see you to my burying, Peter. Lay me in the grave with my face to the east, and put above me Jesus Christ's own watchword, "*Thy kingdom come.*"' After that he asked only for water, and so he died."

"Blessed are such dead. There is no need to weep for them."

"That is one thing sure; but I have seen this, Nanna: that the wicked is unbefriended in his death-pang."

"And after it, David? O David, after it?"

"There is no darkness nor shadow of death where the worker of iniquity may hide," he answered with an awful solemnity.

"O David, we come into the world weeping, and we go out fearing. It is a hard travail, both for body and soul."

And David walked to the little table on which the Book lay, and he turned the leaves until he found the words he wanted. And Nanna watched him with eyes purified by that mysterious withdrawal into the life of the soul which comes through a great sorrow.

"It was not always so, Nanna," he said. "Listen!"

"For their sakes I made the world, and when Adam transgressed my statutes, then was decreed that now is done.

"Then were the entrances of this world made narrow, full of sorrow and travail; they are but few and evil, full of perils and very painful.

"For the entrances of the elder world were wide and sure, and brought immortal fruit.

But yet there is to be a restoration, Nanna."

"I know not," she answered wearily. "It is so far off–so far away."

"But it is promised. It is sure.

"The world shall be turned into the old silence seven days, like as in former judgments, so that no man shall remain.

"And after seven days, the world, that yet awaketh not, shall be raised up; and that shall die that is corrupt.

"And the earth shall restore those that are asleep in her; and the dust, those that dwell in silence; and the secret places shall deliver those souls that were committed unto them.

"And the Most High shall appear upon the seat of judgment, and misery shall pass away, and the long suffering shall have an end.

"But judgment shall remain; truth shall stand; and faith shall wax strong."

"I know nothing of these things, David; I cannot think of them. What I want is some word of comfort about Vala–a little word from beyond would make all the difference. *Why* is it not given? *Why* is there no answering voice from the other side? There is none on this. *Why* does God pursue a poor, broken-hearted woman so hardly? Even now, when I have wept my heart cold and dumb, I do not please him. One thing only is sure–my misery. Oh, *why, why*, David?"

And David could only drop his eyes before the sad, inquiring gaze of Nanna's. He murmured something about Adam and the cross, and told her sorrowfully that He who hung upon it, forsaken, in the dark, also asked, "Why?" The austerity and profound mystery of his creed gave him no more comforting answer to the pathetic inquiry.

He spent the day in the little hamlet, and, the weather being dry and not very cold, he persuaded Nanna to take a walk upon the cliff-top with him. She agreed because she had not the strength to oppose his desire; but if David had had any experience with suffering women, he would have seen at once how ineffectual his effort would be. The gray, icy, indifferent sea had nothing hopeful to say to her. The gray gulls, with their stern, cold eyes, watchful and hungry, filled her ears with nothing but painful clamoring. There was no voice in nature to cry, "Comfort," to a bruised soul.

She said the wind hurt her, that she was tired, that she would rather sit still in the house and shut her eyes and think of Vala. She leaned so heavily on him that David was suddenly afraid, and he looked with more scrutiny into her face. If his eyes had been opened he would have seen over its youth and beauty signs of a hand that writes but once; for when despair assumes the dignity of patience it carries with it the warrant of death.

They went slowly and silently back to the house, and as they approached it David said, "Some one has called, for the door is open." And they walked a little faster, so that Nanna's cheeks flushed with the movement and the wind.

Matilda Sabiston sat on the hearthstone grumbling at the cold, while the man-servant who had brought her so far was piling the peats upon the fire to warm her feet and hands. When David and Nanna entered she did not move, but she turned her eyes upon them with a malignant anger that roused in both a temper very different from that in which their hopeless walk had been taken. It was immediately noticeable in Nanna. She dropped David's hand and walked forward to her visitor, and they looked steadily at each other for a few moments. Then Matilda said:

"Think shame of yourself, to be so soon at the courting again, and, above all, with him!"

Nanna took no notice of the remark, but asked, "Why are you here? I wish to have no dealings with you, for no good can come of them."

"Would I come here for good? There is no good in any of your kind. I came here to tell you that I was glad that there is one Borson less."

"There has been death among your own kin, mistress," said David, "and such death as should make the living fear to bring it to remembrance."

"I know it. You ought to fear. Did you slay Nicol, as your father slew Bele Trenby, by water? or did you poison him with drugs? or is your hand red with his life-blood? And now, before the fish have had time to pick his bones, you are wooing his wife."

"Will you let Nanna alone? She is ill."

"Ill? Babble! Look at her rosy cheeks! She has been listening to your love-words. Who sent you to the *Sea Rover*? What were you doing there? A great plot! A wicked plot against poor Nicol!"

"I went to the *Sea Rover* because—"

"Very ready you were to go to Nicol's ship and to do your will there! Oh, it was a great opportunity! None to see! none to tell tales! But I know you! I know you! The black drop of murder is in every Borson's veins."

"Mistress, you are an old woman, and you may say your say. If you were a man it would be different. I would cut out your lying tongue, or make it eat its own words."

With railing and insolence she defied him to the act, and David stood looking at her with his hands in his pockets. As for Nanna, she had thrown off her cloak and seated herself on Vala's couch. She was trying to control her temper; but the little room was already impregnated with Matilda's personality, and Nanna could not escape from those indirect but powerful influences that distil from an actively evil life.

"I wish, Matilda Sabiston, that you would leave my house," she said. "I think that you have brought the devil in with you."

Then Matilda turned in her chair and looked at Nanna. Her face, handsomely prominent in youth, had become with sin and age like that of a bird of prey; it was all nose and two fierce, gleaming eyes.

"Do you talk of the devil?" she screamed. "You, who drove your husband to sin, and sent your baby to hell!"

Then Nanna, with a pitiful cry, buried her face in Vala's pillow; and David, full of anger, said:

"I will take you from this house, mistress. You were not asked to come here, and you cannot stay here."

"I will stay until I have said what you shall listen to. The child of this woman has been taken for your father's sin. The mother will go next. Then *you* will bite the last morsel of Kol's curse. I am living only to see this."

"I fear not the curse of any man," said David, in a passion. "There is no power in any mortal's curse that prayer cannot wither. Keep it to yourself— you, who believe in it. As for me—"

"As for you, I will give you some advice. When the new minister is placed, go and tell him what Liot Borson told you at his death-hour. For I know well he did not die without boasting of his revenge on Bele Trenby. Death couldn't shut Liot's mouth till the words were out of it. Make the confession your father ought to have made, and let me hear it. I have said it, and fools have laughed at me, and wise men have hid the words in their hearts; and I will not die till my words are made true. And if you will not make them true, then the dead will have their satisfaction, and love will go to the grave and not to the bridal. Now, then, do what is before you. I have set you your task."

She spoke with a rapid passion that would not be interrupted, and then, still muttering threats and accusations, tottered out of the cot on her servant's arm. David was speechless. The truth bound him. What powers of divination this evil woman had, he knew not, but she at least had driven home the unacknowledged fear in his heart. He sat down by Nanna and tried to comfort her, but she could not listen to him. "Leave me alone today," she pleaded. "I have had all I can bear."

So he went back to Lerwick, feeling with every step he took that the task Matilda had set him would have to be accomplished. The humiliation would indeed be great, but if by confession he could ward off punishment from Nanna he must accept the alternative. Himself he took not into consideration. No threat and no fear of personal suffering could have forced him to speak; but if, peradventure, silence was sin, and sin brought sorrow, then his duty to others demanded from him the long-delayed acknowledgment. However, he was not yet certain of the right, and the new minister had not yet come, and there is always some satisfaction in putting off what is dubious and questionable.

The new minister was not finally settled until Christmas. He proved to be a young man with the air of theological schools still around him. David was afraid of him. He thought of the tender, mellowed temper of the old man whose place he was to fill, and wished that his acknowledgment had been made while he was alive. He feared to bring his father's spiritual case before one who had never known him, who had grown up "southward" under very different influences, who would likely be quite unable to go a step beyond the letter of the law.

He talked to Nanna frequently about the matter, and she was more than inclined to silence. "Let well alone, David," she said. "What good can come of calling back old sins and sorrows? Who has set you this task? One who has always hated you. If God had sent, would he have sent by *her*? No; but when the devil wants a cruel, wicked messenger, he can get none so fit for his purpose as a bad old woman."

However, while David hesitated Matilda went to the new minister. She prefaced her story by a gift of ten pounds for the replenishing of the manse, and then told it according to her own wishes and imagination.

"The minister dead and gone would not listen to me," she said. "He was a poor creature, and Liot Borson was one of his pets. The man could do no wrong in his eyes. So I have been sin-bearer for more than twenty years. Now, then, I look to you to clear this matter to the bottom, and let the talk about it come to an end once for all."

"It is a grave matter," said Minister Campbell, "and I am astonished that my predecessor let it rest so long–though doubtless he did it for the best, for there will be two sides to this, as to all other disputes."

"There is not," answered Matilda, angrily. "All is as I have told you."

"But, according to your testimony, Liot Borson's guilt rests on your dreams. That is a poor foundation."

"I have always been a foresighted woman–a great dreamer–and I dream true."

"But I know not how to call a kirk meeting on a dream."

"Was the Bible written for yesterday or for to-day?"

"It was written for every day, unto the end of time."

"Then look to it. Ask it how many of its great events hang upon dreams. Take the dream life out of the Bible, minister, and where are you?"

"Mistress Sabiston, I am not used to arguing with women, but I will remind you that the dream life of the Bible does not rest on female authority. It was the men of the Bible that saw visions and dreamed dreams. As I remember, only one woman–a pagan, Pilate's wife–is recorded as being in this way instructed. I should not be inclined to discipline the memory of Liot Borson on the strength of your dream."

"There is, or there was, other evidence; for much of it has now gone away through the door of death. What I want is Liot's own confession. He made it to his son before he gave up the ghost. Now, then, let David speak for his father."

"That is a different thing. If David has a message to deliver, he must deliver it, or he is recreant to his trust."

"See to it, then. It is all I ask, but I have a right to ask it."

"What right?"

"Bele was my adopted son. I loved him. He was my heir. I was a lone-living woman, and he was all I had. As I have told you, Liot wished to marry my niece Karen, that he might heir my property. He had every reason to get Bele out of his way, and he did it. Ask his son."

"I will."

With these words he became silent, and Matilda saw that there was an end of the conversation for that time. But she was now more eager and passionate for the impeachment of Liot's good name than she had ever been, and she vowed to herself that if Minister Campbell did not give her satisfaction he should have all the petty misery and trouble her money and influence could give him.

The young minister, however, did not hesitate. It was a most unpleasant legacy to his charge, and he was straitened until he had done his duty concerning it. He went to see David at once, and heard from his lips the whole truth. And he was greatly impressed with the story, for the young man told it with such truth and tenderness that every word went heartwise. He could think of nothing better than to call a meeting in the kirk, and summon David to tell the congregation just what he had told him. And as it had been Liot's intention to do this very thing himself, the minister could not see that David would be guilty of any unkindness to his father's memory. Quite the contrary. He would be fulfilling his desire and doing for him the duty he had been unable personally to perform.

David had nothing to say against the proposal. It turned him faint, and he wondered if it would be possible for him to stand up in the presence of his fellows, and in the sight of all the women who admired and respected him, and do what was required. A cold sweat covered his face; his large hands felt powerless; he looked at the minister appealingly, but could not utter a word.

"You must speak for your father, David. Perhaps you ought to have spoken before this. We can do so little for the dead that any wish of theirs that is positive ought to be sacredly granted. What do you say?"

"It is hard, minister. But what you say is right, that I will do."

"We will not touch the Sabbath day, David. I will ask the people to come to the kirk next Wednesday afternoon. The men will not be at sea, and the women will be at leisure then. What do you think?"

PEAT-GATHERERS.

"As you think, minister."

"Tell them just what you have told me. I believe every word you have said, and I will stand by you–I and all good men and women, I am sure."

"Thank you, minister."

But he could scarcely utter the words. He had often thought of this ordeal; now that it was really to face, his heart utterly failed him. He went straight to Nanna, and she forgot her own sorrow in his, and so comforted and strengthened him that he went away feeling that all things would be possible if she was always as kind and sympathetic.

It was then Friday, and Wednesday came inexorably and swiftly. David tried in every way to prepare himself, but no strength came from his efforts. Prayer, nor meditation, nor long memories of the past, nor hopes for the future, had any potency. He was stupefied by the thing demanded of him, and the simple, vivid cry which always brings help had not yet been forced from his lips. But at the last moment it came. Then the coldness and dumbness and wretched inertness that had bound him, body and soul, were gone. When he saw Matilda Sabiston enter the kirk, her eyes gleaming and her face eager with evil expectations, he felt the wondrous words of David[3] burning in his heart and on his lips, and he was no longer afraid. Psalm after psalm went singing through his soul, and he said joyfully to himself, "Sometimes God is long in coming, but he is *never too late.*"

The minister did not ascend the pulpit. He stood at the table, and after a prayer and a hymn he said:

"We have come together this afternoon to hear what David Borson has to say in regard to the charge which Matilda Sabiston has made for twenty-six years against his father Liot Borson."

"That question was decided long ago," said an old man, rising slowly. "I heard Minister Ridlon give verdict concerning it at the funeral of Liot's wife."

"It was *not* decided," cried Matilda, standing up, and turning her face to the congregation. "Liot Borson found it easy to lie at his wife's coffin-side, but when it came to his own death-hour he did not dare to die without telling the truth. Ask his son David."

"David Borson," said the minister, "at your father's death-hour did he indeed confess to the slaying of Bele Trenby?"

Then David stood up. All fear had gone, he knew not where. He looked even taller than his wont. And the light of God's presence was so close to him that his large, fair face really had a kind of luminosity.

"Minister," he answered with a solemn confidence, "minister and friends, my father at his death-hour expressly said that *he did not slay Bele Trenby*. He said that he laid no finger on him, that he fell into his own snare. This is what happened: He met my father on the moss, and said, 'Good evening, Liot.' And my father said, 'It is dark,' and spoke no more. You know—all of you know—they were ill friends and rivals; so, then, silence was the best. And if Bele had been content to be silent and tread slowly in my father's steps he had reached his ship in safety. But he must talk and he must hurry; and the first was not wanted, and the second was dangerous. And after a little my father's shoe-strings came undone, and he stooped to tie them— who wouldn't, where a false step or a fall might be death? And Bele went on, and called back to him, 'Is this the crossing?' And father had not finished fastening his shoes, and did not answer. So then Bele called again, and it is likely father would not be hurried by him, and he did not answer that time, either. And Bele said he was in the devil's temper, and went on at his own risk. And the next moment there was a cry, and my father lifted his head hastily, and the man had walked into the moss, and then who *could* help him? But well I know, if help had been possible, my father would have given his own life to save life, even though the man was ten times his enemy. Over and over I have seen Liot Borson bring from the sea men who hated him, and whom no one else would venture life for. Never mortal man walked closer with God than Liot Borson. I, who have lived alone with him for twenty years, I know this; and I will dare to say that in the matter of Bele Trenby he did no worse, and perhaps a great deal better, than any other man would have done. Why was Bele on the moss? He was a sailor and a stranger. A man must have life-knowledge of the moss to walk it in the night-time. When my father was willing to guide him across it, was it too much that he should be silent, and that he should let his guide do a thing so necessary as to secure tightly his shoes on the soft, unstable ground? Was his guide to let go this safe precaution because Bele was in a hurry to reach his ship? Was Liot Borson to blame if the man's foolhardiness and insolent presumption led him into danger and death? As for me, I say this: I wish to be a man after my father's heart. For he was a righteous man in all his ways, and kind-hearted to every creature in trouble; and he was a life-saver, and not a murderer. And this I, his loving son, will maintain to my last breath. And if, after these words, any man says, 'Liot Borson was a murderer,' I will call him a cowardly liar and slanderer at Lerwick Market Cross, and follow the words to the end they deserve. And God knows I speak the truth, and the whole truth."

Then David sat down, and there was an audible stir and movement of sympathy and approbation. And the minister said: "I believe every word you have spoken, David. If any present has a word to say, now is the time to speak."

Then Elder Hay rose and said: "Of what use is talk? Liot Borson is dead and judged. How shall we, sinful men ourselves, dare to meddle with the verdict of the Lord God Almighty? If we in our ignorance or spite reverse it, what a presumption it will be! And if we confirm it, is God's decree made stronger by our 'yea, yeas'? What at all does Mistress Sabiston want?"

"I want Liot Borson's name taken off the roll," she answered vehemently. "It has no right in the kirk's books. Cross it out! Blot it out! It is a shame to the white pages."

"Is there here any man or woman who will do Mistress Sabiston's will, and cross out Liot Borson's name for her?" asked the minister.

There was a deep, emphatic "No!" And the minister continued: "I would myself rather cut off my right hand than cross out the name of one who has passed far beyond our jurisdiction. Suppose—and we have a right to suppose—that the name of Liot Borson is written in the shining letters of the book of life, and we have crossed it off our kirk book! What then? I think this question is settled. I never want to hear it named again. I will enter into no conversations about it. It has been taken out of our hands by God himself. We will not dare to discuss in any way what he has already decided. We will now sing together the Forty-third Psalm."

And, amid the rustle of the opening leaves, the minister himself started the psalmody. There was a little air of hurry in his movements, as if he hasted to drown all contention in singing; but he had reached his usual grave composure before the end of the verses, and the benediction fell like the final satisfying chords of the melody.

Matilda was dumfounded by such a cutting short of the case, but even she dared not interrupt functions so holy as praise and prayer. In the kirk she was compelled to restrain her indignation, but when she found that the resolution of Minister Campbell not to discuss the matter or enter into any conversation about it was universally adopted by the townspeople, her anger found words such as are not to be met with in books; and she did not spare them.

David was singularly happy and satisfied. He had been grandly supported both by God and man, and he was grateful for the pronounced kindness of his friends, for their hand-shakings and greetings and loving words and wishes. But when both the enthusiasm and the pang of conflict were over, oh, how good it was to clasp Nanna's hand, and in this perfect but silent companionship to walk home with her! Then Nanna made a cup of tea, and they drank it together, and talked over what had been said and done, finally drifting, as they always did, to that invincible necessity that whatever is could not but so have been. And though their words were, as all human words about God must be, terribly inadequate, yet their longing, their love, and their fears were all understood. And He who is so vast and strange when

With intellect we gaze,

Close to their hearts stole in,

In a thousand tender ways.

---

[3]

1 Ps. xxvii.

<hr size=2 width="100%" align=center>

IX
A SACRIFICE ACCEPTED

After this the winter came on rapidly and severely. The seas were dangerous, and the fishing precarious and poor, and the fever still lingered, many cases being found as far north as Yell. Thus suffering and hard poverty and death filled the short days and made twice as long the stretched-out nights of the dark season. The old cloud gathered round David, and when the minister preached of "the will and purposes of God," it seemed to David that they were altogether penal. The unfathomable inner side of his life was all gloom and doubt; how, then, could the material side be cheerful and confident?

The new minister, however, had conceived a strong liking for the young man; they were nearly of the same age; and he saw that David was troubled about spiritual matters, and took every opportunity to discuss them with him. But he had too much of the schools, he was too untried, and had been, in the main, too happily situated to comprehend David's views. The very piety of the two men was different. David's was lively, personal, and tender; it sat in the center. The minister's was official, intellectually accepted, conscientiously practised. It was not strange, then, that any dissent David ventured to make was not conceived of as a soul-query, but rather as a challenge against impregnable truths. He was always ready to defend Calvinism, though David did not consciously attack it. To be sure, he said strange and daring things—things which came from his heart, and which often staggered his opponent; but all the more Minister Campbell put on his armor to defend his creed.

"It is a hard religion for men and for women," said David, as they talked a stormy afternoon away on Barbara's hearthstone; "and why God gave it, I can't tell; for, after all, minister, the blessedness of heaven is an eternity older than the damnation of hell."

"Men called it unto themselves, and it is not hard, David. It is a grand creed; it is a strong anchor for a weak soul; it won't let a man drift into the deep waters of infidelity or the miserable shoals of 'perhaps' and 'suppose.' Neither will it let him float on waves of feeling like Arminianism, and be content with 'ahs' and 'ohs,' and shrink from 'therefores.' Calvinism makes strong men before the Lord, David, and strong men are not laid on rose-leaves and fed on pap and cream."

"That is true, minister; for it seems to me that whenever men are to be fishers, and fight the winds and waves, or to make a living out of bare moor or rocks, or to do any other of the hard work of life, they are born Calvinists."

"Just so, David. Arminians can weave a piece of broadcloth, and Episcopals can till the rich, juicy fields of England; but God's hard work–yes, David, and his hard fighting–has to be done by his Calvinists. They were the only fighting Protestants. But for Calvinists, Puritans, Huguenots, there would have been no Reformation. Philip and the Pope would have had their way, and we should all have been papists or atheists."

"I know not. You say so, minister, and it is doubtless true."

"It is true. You have been born to a noble creed; accept it with thankfulness and without demur. You are not called upon to understand it or to reason about it. It is faith that conquers."

And after such an oration the young minister would go away with a proud sense of duty well performed, burning with his own evangel, and liking David well for being the invoker of his enthusiasm. But David, after his departure, was always silent and depressed; his intellect may have been quickened, but he was not comforted.

The sunshine that had brightened his life during the past year was gone, for he had found out that all his happiness was bound up in Nanna, and Nanna was on the verge of despair. Day by day she grew thinner and whiter, more melancholy and more silent. She did only work enough to supply the barest needs of life, and for the most part sat hour after hour with dropped hands and closed eyes; or she was seized with a restlessness that drove her to motion, and then she walked the small bounds of her room until physical exhaustion threw her into deep sleep.

David watched her with a sad patience. He had felt severely the loss of Vala, and he did not presume to measure Nanna's sorrow by his own. He knew it was natural that for some weeks she should weep for a child so dear, whose little life had been so pitifully wronged, so bound to suffering, so cruelly cut short. But when this natural sorrow was not healed by time, when Nanna nursed her grief to despair and dwelt with it in the valley of the shadow of death, he thought it time to reason with her.

"You will kill yourself, Nanna," he said.

"Well, then, David, I hate life."

"Do you wish to die?"

"No; I am afraid to die. I know that I am sinning every day in weeping for my poor lost bairn, and yet I am that way made that I cannot help but weep for her. For it is my fault, David, all my fault. Why, then, did He pursue the child with His anger from the first hour of her sorrowful life to the last? And where is she now? O David, where is she? If God would only let me go to her!"

"*Whist*, Nanna! You know not what you are saying. You might be asking yourself away from His presence."

"I would rather be with Vala. If that be sinful, let me thole the wages of my sin. Where is my dear bairn?"

"I heard Elder Kennoch say we may have a hope that God will eventually take pity on those babes who have done no actual sin."

"But *when* will he take pity? And until he does, how can the wee souls endure his anger? O David, my heart will break! My heart will break!"

"Nanna, listen to this: when Elga Wick's child died, the minister said there was a benign interpretation of the doctrines which taught us that *none but elect infants died*. It would be unjust, Nanna, unless the child was elect, not to give it the offer of salvation."

"What good would eighty years of 'offers' do, if there was no election to eternal life?"

"Nanna, your father was a child of God, and you have loved him from your youth upward."

"Can that help Vala?"

"Even so. He keeps his mercy for children's children, to the third and fourth generation of them that fear him. Vala was in the direct succession of faith."

"You know what her father and his folk have been?"

"Yes, I know."

"Oh, why did my father let me marry the man? He should rather have tied me hands and feet, and cast me into the depths of the sea. He should have said to me, 'Nanna, you may have a bairn, and it may be a child of sin, and thus foreordained to hell-fire.' Do you think then I would have wed Nicol Sinclair?"

"Ay, I think you would."

"Do you believe that I was born for that end?"

"I think you had set your heart on Nicol at all risks."

"At that time Nicol was in good favor with all folk."

"You have told me that your father liked him not, and that he said many things to you against a marriage with him; so, then, if your heart had not been fully set on its own way, his 'no' would have been sufficient. If we heed not fathers and mothers and teachers, we should not heed, Nanna, no, not if one came from the dead to warn us."

"That is an awful truth, David."

"And one must speak truth to heal a wounded soul. If there be a canker in the body, you know well the doctor must not spare the sharp knife. But I would not put away hope for Vala–no, indeed!"

"Why, David? Oh, why?"

"Has she not kindred in His presence? Will He not remember His promise to them? Will they forget to remind Him of it? I think not so hardly of the dead."

"David, I will tell you the last awful truth. I never could get the poor little one baptized,–things ay went so against it,–and she died without being signed and sealed to His mercy; that is the dreadful part of her death. I was ashamed–I was afraid to tell you before. O David, if you had stayed by Vala instead of going to that man, you might perhaps have won her this saving grace; but it was not to be."

David almost fainted with the shock of this intelligence. He understood now the anguish which was driving Nanna into the grave; and he had no comfort to offer her, for Nanna seemed to make out a terribly clear case of rejection and of foreordained refusal.

"I was feared to ask Nicol to stand with the child when it ought to have been presented in the kirk," she said.

"But your father?" asked David.

"I was feared to ask my father to stand in Nicol's place, lest it should make Nicol harder to me than he was. And," she continued, weeping bitterly as she spoke, "I thought not of Vala dying, and hoped that in the future there might be a way opened. If father had lived he would have seen to the child's right, but he was taken just when he was moving in the matter; and then Nicol grew harder and harder, and as for the kirk, he would not go there at all, and I had no kin left to take his place. Then the child was hurt, and I was long ill, and Nicol went away, and my friends grew cold, fearing lest I might want a little help, and even the minister was shy and far off. So I came out here with my sorrow, and waited and watched for some friend or some opportunity. 'To-morrow, perhaps to-morrow,' I said; but it was not to be."

"Nanna, you should have told me this before. I would have made the promises for Vala; I would have done so gladly. Surely you should have spoken to me."

"Every day I thought about it, and then I was feared for what would happen when Nicol found it out. And do you not think that Matilda Sabiston would have sent him word that I had set you to do his duty? She would have twitted him about it until he would have raged like a roaring lion, and blackened my good name, and yours also, and most likely made it a cause for the knife he was ever so ready to use. And then, David, there are folks—kirk folks, and plenty of them—who would have said, 'There must be something wrong to set Nicol Sinclair to blood-spilling.' And Matilda Sabiston would have spoken out plainly and said, 'There is something wrong'—and this and that, and more to it."

"And well, then?"

"Well, then, being Matilda, no one would have thought of contradicting her; for she gives much money to the kirk and the societies, and has left all she has to free slaves. No; there was nothing to be done but to thole and be quiet."

"There might be some excuse for being quiet when Vala was not in danger, but when her life was going, why did you not send for the minister?"

"This is what happened; for, David, God's will must be done. No one came here but the doctor. On the second day he said, 'She is not very sick.' At his next visit he said, 'She will die.' Then I told him the child was not baptized, and prayed him to go for the minister. And he said he would certainly do so. But he was called here and there, and he forgot that day; and the next morning very early he went to the manse, and the minister had gone away; and the great storm kept him away for three days; so when he got back the message had been overlaid by many others."

"O Nanna! Nanna!"

"Yes, it was so. After the storm the doctor came again, and Vala was dying. And then he rode like a man riding for his life, and spoke very angrily to the minister, who was not to blame at all, and the minister was hurt at his words; but he came that afternoon, and it was *too late*."

"O Nanna! O Vala! Vala! Vala!"

"So the minister was angry with me for my delays, and he spoke the hard truth to me, and every word went to my soul like a sword. I thought I should die that night, and I longed to die. There was no friend to say to me one word of comfort, and I did not dare to pray. I was feared God would ask me, 'Where is your child?' O David, what for at all did God make us?

For this life is full of sorrow, and it is little comfort to be told that there is a worse one after it."

David took her hand, and a tear dropped upon her slender brown fingers; but he did not answer her question. Indeed, he could not. The same bewildering inquiry had haunted his own sad life. So much sorrow and pain, and at the end perhaps to be "hardly saved," while all around innumerable souls were going down, without hope or helper, to eternal wrath! What for at all had God made man for such a fate?

For that he had *not* made man for such ends was a fact outside their understandings, even as a possibility; and its very suggestion at this hour would have appeared to both an impiety of the worst kind. So they consoled each other in the only way possible to souls at once so miserable and so submissive. With clasped hands they wept together over the inscrutable fate which had set them so hard a lesson to learn as life, with so little light to learn it by.

Natural events deepened the gloom of this spiritual thraldom. Storms of unusual severity swept over the bare, brown land, and the fishing was not only dangerous, but often impossible. But David regarded frost and snow, stormy winds and raging seas, poverty, pestilence, and death, as part of the eternal necessity pursuing its never-ending work through discord and imperfection. When there was a possibility of casting the fifty fathoms of ling-lines, David and his helpers were sure to venture out; when it was clearly impossible, he went to Nanna's and sat with her.

To the ordinary observer there did not seem to be pleasure enough in these visits to reward him for the stormy walk over the moor. His clothing was often wet or stiff with frost, or he was breathless with fighting the strong wind, and not infrequently he lost himself in the bewildering snow; but with some trifle in his pocket for Nanna, he always managed to reach her. It might be only a fish, or a loaf of bread which Barbara had baked for her, or a little fresh milk in a bottle; but it was an offering made rich by that true affection which counted weariness rest for her sake.

He generally found her sitting brooding by her peat fire. Now, peat is cheap in Shetland, and Nanna had no stint of the fuel, but it does not make a cheerful fire. Its want of flame and its dull-red glow stimulate sorrowful musing; and as there is little radiation of heat from it, those whom it warms must sit close to its embers. Thus David and Nanna passed many hours of that sad winter. The snow often veiled what light of day there was, and the great sea-winds shrieked around the hut and blew the peat smoke down the chimney into their faces; and there was little warmth or comfort, and none of the pretty accessories that love generally delights in.

But David's love was not dependent upon accidentals. He had seen Nanna when he thought her very finely dressed; he had watched her when she was happy with her child and contented with his friendship; but she was not then more beautiful than she was now, when her eyes were haunted by despairing thoughts, and her face white and sad, and her noble form was shrouded rather than dressed in the black gown of her loss and woe.

To David she was ever Nanna. It was the woman beneath the outward form he desired—the woman whose tears and fears and wounded love were part of his own sufferings, whose despair was his despair, whose personality, even, affected something far deeper and chaster than that physical emotion too often misnamed love. He knew that he could live for her, however sorrowful life might be; he knew that he could gladly die for her, if his death could bring her spiritual peace or hope.

Thus, in the red light of the glowing peats, with the stormy world around them, to David and Nanna the winter months wore away. When Nanna was able to weep she was then at her best—the most companionable, the most grateful, and the most affectionate. And few would think such circumstances favorable to the growth of love; but that is a great mistake. Love is not perfect love until it has been watered again and again with tears.

Of the growth of this affection it is not likely either was quite unaware; but there is an instinctive dislike in a pure heart to investigate the beginnings of love. It is like laying bare the roots of a flower to see how it grows. And in Nanna's case there was even a fear of such a condition. Love had brought her only heartbreak and despair. Without deliberate intention, she yet grew a little more shy of David; she began to restrain spiritual confidence and to weep alone. He was not slow to feel the change, and it depressed him, and made Barbara wonder at Nanna's ingratitude and womanish unreason.

"A good man fretting for her love, when there are hearts and hearts full waiting for his asking," she said to her neighbor Sally Groat.

And Sally answered: "Well, well, there is a fool in every one's sleeve sometimes; and David Borson is that daft about blood-kin, there is no talking to him. But this is what I say: for all your kindred, make much of your friends—and a friend you have been to him, Barbara."

"Well, then, I have done my best; and friends are to be taken with their faults. To-day I shall talk to David; for the spring comes on so quickly, and I heard that my son's ship had been spoke in the Iceland seas."

"It is long now since Nanna's baby died, and she still weeps without end for her. She ought to try and forget. It was but a sickly child, and never like to be world-wise or world-useful."

"I wouldn't say such words, Sally," answered Barbara, with some warmth. "No one can tell a mother, 'Thy heart shall not remember.' I have laid in earth five children, and do you think I ever slunk away from heartache by forgetting them? No, indeed! I would have counted *that* treason against my own soul."

"God's blessing! there is none wants to contradict you, Barbara. Don't be so hasty, woman. But you know there has been death and weeping in many houses besides Nanna's this winter."

"To be sure," acknowledged Barbara. "Death has asked no man's leave to enter; he has gone into the rich man's house as well as into poor Nanna's hut."

"Every door is wide enough for a coffin."

"Yes; and the minister said last Sabbath that it was this which dissatisfied us with these habitations of clay, and made us lift our eyes to those eternal in the heavens."

"Well, then, to come back to David," said Sally, "he is good, and able to marry. He has saved money, no doubt. Some young men spend their last bawbee, and just live between ebb and flow. That isn't David Borson. Besides, Barbara, you ought to tell him how people are talking."

"I may do that. David is imprudent, and Nanna is too miserable to care. Well, then, those who kindle the fire must put up with the smoke; yet, for all that, I shall have a word or two for him, and that very soon."

David had been at sea all night, and while this conversation was going on he was sleeping; but in the afternoon, as Barbara saw him preparing to go to Nanna's, she said:

"Stay a minute, David Borson. I want to speak to you. I had good news early this morning. My son's ship was met not so far away, and he may get home at any time, and me not thinking of it."

"I am glad to hear it, Barbara. Then, also, you will want my room. I must look for a new place, and that is bad for me."

"I was thinking of Nanna Sinclair," said Barbara, in a musing manner. "People do talk about you and her. I have heard say—"

"'I have heard say' is half a lie," answered David.

"I think that too; but Nanna's good name is to be thought of, and a man does not go every day to see a woman for nothing."

Then David leaped to his feet with a face like a flame. "The shortest and best answer is doing the thing," he muttered; and he walked straight to

Nanna's house, telling himself as he went, "I have been too long about it; I must speak now, and she must answer me."

He was in his fishing-garb, for he intended going to sea with the tide then rising; but he thought no more of dressing for the interview than he thought of preparing his speeches. Hitherto he had in a manner drifted with the current of his great affection, never consciously asking himself where it was bearing him; but if people were talking about Nanna, then he must take away all occasion for suspicion—he must at once ask Nanna to be his wife. And as soon as he took the first step toward her he felt how close and dear she had become to him. He knew then that if Nanna was lost all the world would be nothing. She had grown into his life as the sea and the stars had grown, and he shrank from any thought that could imply separation. He walked with rapid steps across the moor, feeling dimly the beauty of the spring afternoon, with its haze of gold and purple on the horizon, where the gray clouds opened out in wistful stretches of daffodil skies.

The door of Nanna's house stood open, and the wind, full of the sharp salt savor of the sea, blew life into the little room. Nanna was busy with her knitting, and the soft, lace-like shawl lay upon her knee. David shut the door and went to her side. His heart was too full to hesitate or to choose words; the simplest were the best.

"Nanna, I have found out that I love you," he said. "Nanna, dearest woman, do you hear me?"

Then her cheeks burned rosy, and she looked at David, and her hands trembled, and the work fell from them.

"Love me a little, my dear! Love me, Nanna!"

"I do love you, David. Who in all the world have I but you?" And the beautiful woman stood up, and he took her within his arms and kissed her.

For a moment or two David was happy. His large, fair face shone; he laughed softly as he drew Nanna to his breast. He was really as intoxicated with joy as some men are with wine.

"We will be married next week, Nanna," he said; "this week—to-morrow, if you will. It has come to this: I must leave Barbara, and there is a house empty close to the quay, and it shall be our home, Nanna; for I have sixty pounds, my dear woman, and at last, at last—"

Before he reached this point he was sensible of some chill or dissent, but he was not prepared for Nanna's answer:

"David, why do you talk of marrying? It is ever that. I will not marry."

"Not yet, Nanna? Is it too soon? But why for a dead man will you keep me waiting?"

"I think not of any dead man."

"Is it Vala? Vala would rejoice in our happiness."

"I will not marry—no, not any man living."

"Why did you say that you loved me?"

"I do love you."

"No; you do not."

He put her gently away from him, and looked at her with a somber sternness. "You do not love me," he continued. "If you did, you would put me first; you would say, 'I will be your wife.' You would delight to make me happy—I, who have never been happy but in sharing your joys and sorrows."

"O David, I do love you!"

"Then be my wife."

"I cannot! I cannot!"

"Then you love me as light, vain women love: to make slaves of men, and bring them back and back to be hurt. It is not to be so with me. No, indeed! Farewell, Nanna."

His voice failed him. He turned toward the door, and for a moment Nanna could not realize that he was actually bidding her a final farewell. When she did she flew to his side, and arrested his hand as he was opening the door.

"Come back! Come back, David!" she entreated. "You are all wrong; you are very cruel to me. If you leave me it will break my heart! It will be the last blow, David. It is the very truth."

He hesitated enough to make Nanna weep with passionate distress, and this emotion he was not able to bear. He took her within his arm again, led her to a chair, and sat down at her side, and as he kissed the tears from her face said:

"If indeed you do love me, Nanna—"

"*If* I do love you!" she interrupted. "I love none but you. You are heart of my heart and soul of my soul. I hear you coming when you are half a mile away. I have no joy but when you are beside me. I shall die of grief if you leave me in anger. I would count it heaven and earth to be your wife, but I dare not! I dare not!"

She was sobbing piteously when she ended this protestation, and David comforted her with caresses and tender words. "What fears you, Nanna?" he asked. "Oh, my dear, what fears you?"

"This is what I fear," she answered, freeing herself from his embrace, and looking steadily at him. "This is what I fear, David. If we were married I might have another child–I might have many children."

Then he clasped her hand tightly, for he began to see where Nanna was leading him, as she continued with slow solemnity:

"Can you, can the minister, can any human being, give me assurance they will be elect children? If you can, I will be your wife to-morrow. If you cannot, as the God of my father lives, I will not bring sons and daughters into life for sin and sorrow here, and for perdition hereafter. The devil shall not so use my body! To people hell? No; I will not–not even for your love, David!"

Her words, so passionate and positive, moved him deeply. He was the old David again–the light, the gladness, all but the tender, mournful love of the past, gone from his face. He held both her hands, and he looked down at them lying in his own as he answered:

"Both of us are His children, Nanna. We are His by generations and by covenant. He has promised mercy to such. Well, then, we may have a reasonable hope–"

"Hope! No, no, David! I must have something better than hope. I hoped for Vala, and my hope has been my hell. And as for the child–my God! where is the child?"

"We love God, Nanna, and the children of the righteous–"

"Are no safer than the children of the wicked, David. I have thought of this continually. There was John Beaton's son; he killed a man, and died on the gallows-tree, to the shame and the heartbreak of his good father and mother. The lad had been baptized, too,–given to God when he drew his first breath,–and God must have rejected him. Minister Stuart's son forged a note, and was sent with felons across the sea. His father and mother had prayed for him all the days of his life; he was brought to the kirk and given to God in baptism; and God must have rejected him also. Think of good Stephen and Anna Blair's children. Their daughter's name cannot be spoken any more, and their sons are bringing down their gray hairs with sorrow to the grave–with sorrow and shame too. Go through the whole kirk, the whole town, the islands themselves, and you will be forced to say, David, that it is the children of the righteous that go to the devil."

"Nanna! Nanna!"

"It is the truth, David. How the good God can treat his bairns so, I know not; but you and I may also deserve his wrath in like manner. I am feared to hope different. O David, I am feared to be a mother again!"

"Nanna! Nanna! what can I say?"

"There is nothing to say. If I should meet Vala in that place where infants 'earnestly desire to see and love God, and yet are not able to do so,' I should cover my face before the child. If she blamed me, I should shiver in speechless agony; if she did not blame me, it would be still harder to bear. Were we only sure–but we are not sure."

"*We are not sure.*" David repeated the words with a sad significance. Nanna's argument, evolved from her own misery and illustrated by that misery, had been before David's eyes for months. He could not escape from such reasoning and from such proof, and his whole life, education, and experience went to enforce the pitiful dilemma in which their love had placed them.

"It is His will, and we must bear it to the uttermost," continued Nanna, with a sorrowful resignation.

"I am very wretched, Nanna."

"So am I, David, very wretched indeed. I used to think monks and nuns, and such as made a merit of not marrying, were all wrong; maybe they are nearer right than we think for. Doubtless they have a tender conscience toward God, and a tender conscience is what he loves."

Then David rose from Nanna's side and walked rapidly to and fro in the room. Motion helped him to no solution of the tremendous difficulty. And Nanna's patient face, her fixed outward gaze, the spiritual light of resolute decision in her eyes, gave to her appearance an austere beauty that made him feel as if this offering up of their love and all its earthly sweetness was a sacrifice already tied to the horns of the altar, and fully accepted.

Now, the law of duty lay very close to David's thoughts; it was an ever-present consciousness, haunting his very being; but the sensual nature always shrinks away from it. David sat down and covered his face with his hands, and began to weep–to sob as strong men sob when their sorrow is greater than they can bear; as they never sob until the last drop, the bitterest drop of all, is added–the belief that God has forsaken them. This was the agony which tore David's great, fond heart in two. It forced from him the first pitiful words of reproach against his God:

"I was sure at last that I was going to be happy, and God is not willing. From my youth up he has ay laid upon me the rod of correction. I wish that I had never been born!"

"My poor lad! but you are not meaning it." And Nanna put her arms around his neck and wept with him. For some minutes he let her do so, for he was comforted by her sympathy; but at last he stood up, passed his hand across his eyes, and said as bravely as he could:

"You are right, Nanna. If you feel in this way, I dare not force your conscience. But I must go away until I get over the sore disappointment."

"Where will you go to, David?"

"Who can tell? The countries in which I may have to earn and eat my bread I know not. But if I was seeing you every day, I might get to feel hard at God."

"No, no! He fashioned us, David, and he knows what falls and sore hurts we must get before we learn to step sure and safe."

"In the end it may all be right. I know not. But this I know: pain and cold and hunger and weariness and loneliness I have borne with a prayer and a tight mouth, and I have never said before that I thought him cruel hard."

"His ways are not cruel, my dear love; they are only past our finding out. The eternal which makes for righteousness cannot be cruel. And if we could see God with our eyes, and hear him with our ears, and understand him with our reason, what grace would there be in believing in him? Did not the minister say last Sabbath that our life was hid with Christ in God, and that therefore God must first be pierced ere we could be hurt or prejudiced? Then let us take what comfort we can in each other's affection, David, and just try and believe that God's ways are the very best of all ways for us."

"Sometime—perhaps—"

"And don't leave me, David. I can bear all things if you are near to help and comfort me."

"Ay, ay; but women are different. I cannot fight the temptation when I am in it; I must run away from it. Farewell! Oh, dear, dear Nanna, farewell!"

He kissed the words upon her lips, and went hastily out of the house; but when he had walked about one hundred yards he returned. Nanna had thrown herself despairingly upon the rude couch made for Vala, and on which the child had spent most of her life. There Nanna lay like one dead. David knelt down by her; he took her within his arms, kissed her closed eyes, and murmured again upon her lips his last words of love and sorrow. Her patient acceptance of her hard lot made him quiver with pain, but he knew well that for a time, at least, they must each bear their grief alone.

Nanna's confession of her love for him had made everything different. In her presence now he had not the power to control his longing for reciprocal affection. He felt already a blind resentment and rebellion against fate—a sense of wrong, which it was hard to submit to. But how could he fight circumstances whose foundations were in eternity? At this hour, at least, he had come to the limit of his reason and his endurance. Again and again he kissed Nanna farewell, and it was like tearing his life asunder when he put away her clinging arms and left her alone with the terrible problem that separated their lives.

There is something worse than the pang of keenest suffering—the passive state of a subjugated heart. A dismal, sullen stillness succeeded to David's angry sorrow. He avoided Barbara and shut himself in his room. And his strong and awful prepossession in favor of the Bible led him, first of all, to go to the book. But he found no help there. His soul was tossed from top to bottom, and he was vanquished by the war in his own bosom. For in our wrestling alone angels do not always come. And David brought his dogmas over and over to the Scriptures, and was crushed spiritually between them, so that at last, worn out with the mental and heart struggle, he submitted to the fatality he could not alter.

"I will go the right road," he said, "however cruel that road may be. Then death may give me back to God a miserable man, but not a guilty one."

And he did not comprehend that, in thus preferring an unseen duty because it was right to a seen pleasure because it was pleasant, he was consummating that sublime act of faith whose cry of victory is, "Thy will be done."

Nanna did not suffer so much. In the first place, the pale, sad, almost despairing woman was glad and dared, in her despair, because the man she loved durst not sin, even for her. In the second, her battle was practically over. She had been in the van of it for months, and had come gradually to that state of submission which fears to resist, lest resistance might be found to be fighting against God. While David was yet in an agony of struggle with his love and his desires, his tender conscience and his dread of offending the Deity, Nanna had washed away her tears, and was strengthening her heart by saying continually, as the glancing needles glided to and fro:

My God and Father, while I stray

Far from my home, on life's rough way,

Oh, teach me from my heart to say,

"Thy will be done!"

For some dauntless, primitive confidence in the love of the Maker of men is older than any creed. And there were yet hours when Nanna's soul outleaped its mortal shadow and had mystic flashes, native and sweet, beyond the reach of will and endeavor–intimations of serenities and compensations which would be neither small nor long delayed.

X
IN THE FOURTH WATCH

Holding despair at bay, David quickly made his preparations for an extended absence. He hired his boat and lines to Groat's sons, and on the morning of the second day, after bidding Nanna farewell, he went to Minister Campbell's to complete his arrangements. The minister was writing his sermon, and he was not pleased at the interruption; but when he saw David's face, the shadow of annoyance on his own passed away like a thought. He dropped his pen, and turned in his chair so as to see the young man fairly, and then he asked:

"What is wrong, David?"

"I am all at sea, minister, drifting–drifting–"

"Where's your anchor, David? Can't you steady yourself on God? Can't you make harbor someway?"

David shook his head sadly.

"Then up sail and out to sea, and face the storm. What quarter is it from?"

"It comes from a woman."

"Ah, David, that is bad to buffet. I have been through it. It was that storm which brought me here. I know all about it."

GROAT.

"Please, minister, I think not. It is Nanna Sinclair."

"I thought so. You love her, David?"

"Better than my life."

"And she does not love you?"

"She loves me as I love her."

"Then what is there to make you miserable? In a few months, David, you will marry her and be happy."

"Nanna will not marry me in a few months–she will not marry me at all."

"Nanna ought not to trouble a good man with such threats. Of course she will marry. Why not?"

Then David told the minister "why not." He listened at first with incredulity, and then with anger. "Nanna Sinclair is guilty of great presumption," he answered. "Why should she sift God's ordination and call in question results she is not able to understand? Marriage is in the direct command of God, and good men and women innumerable have obeyed the command without disputing. It is Nanna's place to take gratefully the love God has sent her—to obey, and not to argue. Obedience is the first round of the ascending ladder, David; and when any one casts it off, he makes even the commencement of spiritual life impossible."

He spoke rapidly, and more as if he was trying to convince himself than to console David. His words, in any case, made no impression. David listened in his shy, sensitive, uncomplaining way, but the minister was quite aware he had touched only the outermost edge of feeling. David's eyes, usually mild and large, had now his soul at their window. It was not always there, but when present it infected and went through those upon whom it looked. The minister could not bear the glance. He rose, and gently pushed David into a chair, and laid his hands on his shoulders, and looked steadily at him. He could see that a gap had been made in his life, and that the bright, strong man had emerged from it withered and stricken. He sat down by his side and said:

"Talk, David. Tell me all."

And David told him all, and the two men wept together. Yet, though much that David said went like a two-edged sword through the minister's convictions, he resented the thrust, and held on to his stern plan of sin and retribution like grim death, all the more so because he felt it to be unconsciously attacked. And when David said: "It is the Shorter Catechism, minister; it is a hard book for women and bairns, and I wonder why they don't teach them from the Scriptures, which are easy and full of grace," the answer came with a passionate fervor that was the protest for much besides the catechism.

"David! David! You must say nothing against the Shorter Catechism. It is the Magna Charta of Calvinism, and woe worth the day for dear old Scotland when its silver trumpet shall no longer be heard and listened to. Its rules and bonds and externals are all very necessary. Believe me, David, few men would remain religious without rules and bonds and externals."

"I am, as I said, minister, all at sea. I find nothing within my soul, nothing within my life-experience, to give me any hope, and I am going away a miserable man."

"David, your hope is not to be grounded on anything within yourself or your life-experience. When you wish to steady your boat, do you fix your anchor on anything within it, or do you cast your anchor outside?"

"I cast it out."

"So the soul must cast out its anchor, and lay hold, not on anything within itself, but on the hope set before it. The anchor of your boat often drags, David, and you drift in spite of it, for there is no sure bottom; but the soul that anchors on the truth of God, the immutability of his counsels, the faithfulness of his promises, is surely steadfast. For I will tell you a great thing, David: God has given us this double guaranty—he has not only said, but sworn it."

Thus the two men talked the morning away. Then David remembered that he had come specially to ask the minister to write out his will and take charge of the money he would leave behind and the rents accruing from the hire of his boat and lines. There was nothing unusual in this request. Minister Campbell had already learned how averse Shetlanders are to having dealings with a lawyer, and he was quite willing to take the charge David desired to impose upon him.

"I may not come back to Shetland," David said. "My father went away and never returned. I am bound for foreign seas, and I may go down any day or night. All I have is Nanna's. If she is sick or in trouble, you will see to her relief, minister. And if I come not back in five years, sell the boat and lines and make over all to Nanna Sinclair."

Then a writing was drawn up to this effect; and David brushed the tears from his eyes with his right hand, and put it, wet with them, into the minister's. He had nothing more to say with his lips, but oh, how eloquent were his great, sad, imploring eyes! They went together to the manse door, and then the minister followed him to the gate of the small croft. And as they stood, one on either side of it, David murmured:

"Good-by, minister."

"Good-by, David, and see that you don't think hardly of either your God or your creed. Your God will be your guide, even unto death; and as for your creed, whatever faults men may find in it, this thing is sure: Calvinism is the highest form ever yet assumed by the moral life of the world."

The next morning, in the cold white light of the early dawn, David left Lerwick. The blue moon was low in the west, the mystery and majesty of earth all around him. At this hour the sea was dark and quiet, the birds being still asleep upon their rocky perches, and the only noise was the flapping of the sails, and the water purring softly with little treble sounds among the clincher chains and against the sides of the boat. David was a passenger on the mail-boat. He had often seen her at a distance, but now, being on board, he looked her over with great interest. She seemed to be nearly as broad as she was long, very bluff at the bows, and so strongly built that he involuntarily asked the man at the wheel: "What kind of seas at all is this boat built for?"

"She's built for the Pentland Firth seas, my lad, *weather permitting*. And there's no place on God's land or water where them two words mean so much; for I can tell you, weather *not* permitting, even this boat couldn't live in them."

Gradually David made his way to Glasgow, and from Glasgow to London. Queen Victoria had then just been crowned, and one day David saw her out driving. The royal carriage, with its milk-white horses, its splendid outriders and appointments, and its military escort, made a great impression on him, but the fair, girlish face of the young, radiant queen he never forgot. Hitherto kings and queens had been only a part of his Bible history; he had not realized their relation to his own life. Shetland was so far from London that newspapers seldom reached Lerwick. Politics were no factor in its social or religious life. The civil lords came to try criminal cases, but the minister was the abiding power. Until David saw the young queen he had not heard of her accession to the throne, but with the first knowledge of her "right" there sprang up in his heart the loyalty she claimed. Had any one asked him in that hour to enter her service, he would have stepped on board her war-ships with the utmost enthusiasm.

But nobody did ask him, and he found more commonplace employment on the *Elizabeth*, a trig, well-built schooner, trading to the Mediterranean for fruits and other products of the Orient. The position was the very one his father had so earnestly desired. Touching first at one historic city and then at another, living in the sunshine, and seeing the most picturesque side of civilization, David added continually to the store of those impressions which go to make up the best part of life.

The captain of the *Elizabeth* owned the vessel and was very fond of her; consequently he was not long in finding out the splendid sea qualities of the young Shetlander. On the fourth voyage he made David his mate, and together they managed the *Elizabeth* so cleverly that she became famous for her speed and good fortune. It was indeed wonderful to see what consciousness and sympathy they endowed her with.

"*Elizabeth* is behaving well," the captain said one morning, as he watched her swelling canvas and noted her speed.

"There isn't much sea on," answered David; "hardly more than what we used to call in Shetland 'a northerly lipper.' But yet I don't like the look to the east'ard and the nor'ard."

"Nor I. You had better tell *Elizabeth*. Talk to her, David; coax her to hurry and get out of the bay. Promise her a new coat of paint; say that I think of having her figurehead gilded."

David was used to hearing *Elizabeth* treated as if she were a living, reasonable creature, but he always smiled kindly at the imputation; it touched something kindred in his own heart, and he replied:

"She'll do her best if she's well handled. It's her life as well as ours, you know."

"It is; anybody knows that. If you ever went into shipping and insurance offices, David, you would hear even landsmen say so. They make all their calculations on the average *life* of a ship. My lad, men build her of wood and iron, but there is something more in a good ship than wood and iron."

"Look to the east, captain."

Then there was the boatswain's whistle, and the shout of sailormen, and the taking in of sails, and that hurrying and scurrying to make a ship trig which precedes the certain coming of a great storm. And the Bay of Biscay is bad quarters in any weather, but in a storm it defies adequate description. When the wind has an iron ring and calls like a banshee, and the waves rise to its order as high as the masthead, then God help the men and ships on the Bay of Biscay!

Five days after the breaking of this storm the *Elizabeth* was sorely in need of such potential help. Her masts were gone, the waves were doubling over her, and her plunges were like the dive of a whale. At the wheel there was a man lashed,—for the hull was seldom above water,—and this man was David Borson. He was the only sailor left strong enough for the work, and he was at the last point of endurance. The icy gusts roared past him; the spray was like flying whiplashes; and it was pitiful to see David, with his bleeding hands on the wheel, stolidly shaking his head as the spray cut him.

He had been on deck for forty hours, buffeted by the huge waves, and he was covered with salt-water boils. His feet were flayed and frozen, and his hands so gashed that he dared not close or rest them, lest the agony of unclasping or moving them again should make him lose his consciousness. He feared, also, that his feet were so badly frozen that he would never be able to walk on them any more. These miseries others were sharing with him; but David had been struck by a falling spar at the beginning of the storm, and there was now an abscess forming on his lung that tortured him beyond his usual speechless patience. "God pity me!" he moaned. "God pity me!"

When the storm ceased the *Elizabeth* was as bare as a newly launched hull, and wallowing like a soaked log. David had fallen forward on his face, and was asleep or insensible. He did not hear the handspike thumped upon the deck, and the cry, "*On deck! on deck! Lord help us! she is going down!*" But some one lifted him on to a raft which had been hastily lashed together, and the misery that followed was only a part of some awful hours when physical pain from head to feet drove him to the verge of madness. He never knew how long it was before they were met by the *Alert*, a large passenger packet going into the port of London, and taken on board. Four of the men were then dead from exhaustion, and the physician on the *Alert* looked doubtfully at David's feet.

"But he is dying," he said, "and why give him further pain?"

Then a young man stepped forward and looked at David. There was both pity and liking in his face, and he stooped, and said something in the dying man's ear. A faint smile answered the words; and the youth spoke to the doctor, and both of them went to work with a will. The effort, even then so desperate, was ere long complicated by fever and delirium, and when David came to himself it was almost like a new birth. He was weaker than an infant—too weak, indeed, to wonder or speculate, or even remember.

He only knew that he was in a large room and that two men were with him. One was at his bedside, quiet and drowsy; the other was reading in a Bible, sitting close by the shaded candle. David knew it was a Bible. Who does not know a Bible, even afar off? No matter how it may be bound, the book has a homely and familiar look that no other book has. David shut his eyes again after seeing it; he felt as safe and happy as if a dear friend had spoken to him. And in a few days the man with the Bible began to come near him, and to read softly the most tender and gracious words he could find in that tenderest of all books.

This was the beginning of an interval of delicious rest to David. It was as if some strong angel swung and hushed and wrapped him in a drowsy, blissful torpor. He felt no pain, not even in his tortured feet, and his hands lay at rest upon the white coverlet, healed of all their smarting and aching. For once in his hard life they were not tired or sore. He knew that he was fed and turned, that his pillows were made soft and cool, and that there was the vague sense of kind presence about him; that sometimes he heard, like a heavenly echo, words of comfort that he seemed to have heard long ago; that he slept and wakened, and slept again, with a conscious pleasure in the transitions.

And he asked no questions. He was content to let life lie in blissful quiescence, to be still, and keep his eyes closed to the world, and his ears deaf to its cries. Gradually these sensations increased in strength. One day he heard his nurse say that it would be well to remove him into an entirely fresh room. And he knew that he was lifted in strong arms, and anon breathed a clearer atmosphere, and slept a life-giving sleep. When he awoke he had new strength. He voluntarily opened his eyes, and saw a tree waving branches covered with fresh, crinkly leaves before his window. It was like a glimpse of heaven. And that afternoon his preserver came to his side and said:

"Thee is much better. Can thee listen to me now?"

Then David looked at the young man and smiled; and their eyes met, and their hands met, and the well man stooped to the sick man and kissed his cheek.

"I am Friend John Priestly," he said. "What is thy name?"

"David–David Borson–Shetland."

"David, thee is going to live. That is good news, is it not?"

"No; life is hard–cruel hard."

"Yes, but thee can say, 'The Lord is mine helper.' Thee can pray now?"

"I have no strength."

"If thee cannot speak, lift up thy hand. He will see it and answer thee."

And David's face shadowed, and he did not lift up his hand; also, if the whisper in his heart had been audible, John Priestly would have heard him say, "What is the use of prayer? The Lord has cast me off."

But John did not try the strength of his patient further at that time. He sat by his side, and laid his hand upon David's hand, and began to repeat in a slow, assuring voice the One Hundred and Third Psalm. Its familiar words went into David's ears like music, and he fell sweetly asleep to its promises. For, though men in their weakness and haste are apt to say, "The Lord hath forgotten to be gracious," they who have but once felt his love, though dimly and far off, cannot choose but trust in it, even to the grave.

And souls fraternize in their common exile. John Priestly loved the young man whom he had saved, and David felt his love. As he came fully back to life the past came clearly back to memory. He remembered Nanna as those who love white jasmine remember it when its starry flowers are gone–with a sweet, aching longing for their beauty and perfume. He remembered those terrible days when physical pain had been acute in every limb and every nerve, when he had fainted with agony, but never complained. He remembered his lonely journey to the grave's mouth, and the dim human phantoms who had stood, as it were, afar off, and helped and cheered him as best they could. And he understood that he had really been born again: a new lease of life had been granted him, and he had come back to earth, as so many wish to come back, with all his old loves and experiences to help him in the future.

If only God would love him! If only God would give him ever so small a portion of his favor! If he would only let him live humbly before him, with such comfort of home and friends as a poor fisherman might have! He wondered, as he lay still, what he or his fathers had done that he should be so sorely punished. Perhaps he had shown too great partiality to his father's memory in the matter of Bele Trenby. Well, then, he must bear the consequences; for even at this hour he could not make up his mind to blame his father more than his father had blamed himself.

And as he lay watching the waving of the green trees, and inhaling the scent of the lilies and violets from the garden below him, he began to think of Shetland with a great longing. The bare, brown, treeless land called him with a hundred voices, and thoughts of Nanna came like a small bird winging the still, blue air. For sorrow can endear a place as well as joy; and the little hut on the bare moor, in which he could see Nanna working at her braiding or her knitting, was the spot on all the earth that drew his soul with an irresistible desire.

Oh, how he wanted to see Nanna! Oh, how he wanted to see her! Just to hold her hand, and kiss her face, and sit by her side for an hour or two! He did not wish either her conscience or his own less tender, but he thought that now, perhaps, they might be cousins and friends, and so comfort and help each other in the daily trials of their hard, lonely lives.

One day, when he was much stronger, as he sat by the open window thinking of these things, John Priestly came to read to him. John had a faculty of choosing the sweetest and most comfortable portions of the Book in his hand. This selection was not without purpose. He had learned from David's delirious complainings the intense piety of the youth, and the spiritual despair which had intensified his sufferings. And he hoped God, through him, would say a word of comfort to the sorrowful heart. So he chose, with the sweet determination of love, the most glorious and the most abounding words of the divine Father.

David listened with a reserved acceptance. It was in a measure a new Scripture to him. It appeared partial. When John read, with a kind of triumph, that the Lord "is long-suffering to us-ward, not willing that *any* should perish, but that *all* should come to repentance," David made a slight movement of dissent; and John asked:

"Is not that a noble love? Thee believes in it, David?"

"No."

The word was softly but positively uttered.

"What then, David?"

"'Some men and angels are predestined unto everlasting life, and others foreordained to everlasting death; and their number is so certain and definite that it cannot be either increased or diminished.'" And David quoted these words from the Confession of Faith with such confidence and despair that John trembled at them.

"David! David!" he cried. "Jesus Christ came to seek and to save the lost."

"It is impossible for the lost to be saved," answered David, with a somber confidence; "only the elect, predestined to salvation."

"And the rest of mankind, David? what of them?"

"God has been pleased to ordain them to wrath, that his justice may be satisfied and glorified."

"David, who made thee such a God as this? Where did thee learn about him? How can thee love him?"

"It is in the Confession of Faith. And, oh, John Priestly, I do love him! Yes, I love him, though he has hid his face from me and, I fear, cast me off forever."

"Dear heart," said John, "thee is wronging thy best Friend."

"If I could think so! Oh, if I could think so!"

"Well, then, as we are inquiring after God, and nothing less, is it not fair to take him at his own word?"

David looked inquiringly at John, but made no answer.

"I mean, will it not be more just to believe what God says of himself than to believe what men,–priests,–long ago dead, have said about him?"

"I think that."

Then, one after another, the golden verses, full of God's love, dropped from John's lips in a gracious shower. And David was amazed, and withal a little troubled. John was breaking up all his foundations for time and for eternity. He was using the Scriptures to grind to powder the whole visible church as David understood it. It was a kind of spiritual shipwreck. His slow nature took fire gradually, and then burned fiercely. Weak as he was, he could not sit still. John Priestly was either a voice in the wilderness crying "Peace!" and "Blessing!" to him, or he was the voice of a false prophet crying "Peace!" where there was no peace. He looked into the face of this new preacher, frank and glowing as it was, with inquiry not unmixed with suspicion.

"Well, then," he cried, "if these things be so, let God speak to me. Bring me a Bible with large letters. I want to see these words with my eyes, and touch them with my fingers."

The conversation thus begun was constantly continued, and David searched the Scriptures from morning to night. Often, as the spring grew fairer and warmer, the two young men sat in the garden with the Bible between them; and while the sunshine fell brightly on its pages they reasoned together of fate and free will, and of that divine mercy which is from everlasting to everlasting. For where young men have leisure spiritual things employ them much more frequently than is supposed. Indeed, it is the young who are most earnestly troubled about the next life; the middle-aged are too busy with this one, and the aged do not speculate, because they will soon know.

Thus, daily, little by little, through inlets and broader ways known only to God and himself, the light grew and grew unto perfect day, and flooded not only the great hills and promontories of his soul, but also shone into all its secret caves and gloomy valleys and lonely places. Then David knew how blind and ignorant he had been; then he was penetrated with loving amazement, and humbled to the dust with a sense of the wrong he had done the Father of his spirit; and he locked himself in his room, and fell down on his face before his God. But into that awful communion, in which so much was confessed and so much forgiven, it is not lawful to inquire.

XI
THE LOWEST HELL

After this the thought of Nanna became an irresistible longing. He could not be happy until she sat in the sunshine of God's love with him. He went into the garden and tested his strength, and as soon as he was in the open air he was smitten with a homesickness not to be controlled. He wanted the sea; he wanted the great North Sea; he longed to feel the cradling of its salt waves under him; and the idea of a schooner reefed down closely, and charging along over the stormy waters, took possession of him. Then he remembered the fishermen he used to know–the fishermen who peopled the desolate places of the Shetland seas.

"I must go home!" he said with a soft, eager passion. "I must go home to Shetland." And there was in his voice and accent that pride and tenderness with which one's home should be mentioned in a strange land.

When he saw John next he told him so, and they began to talk of his life there. John had never asked him of his past. He knew him to be a child of God, however far away from his Father, and he had accepted his spiritual brotherhood with trustfulness. He understood that it was David's modesty that had made him reticent. But when David was ready to leave he also felt that John had a right to know what manner of man he had befriended. So, as they sat together that night, David began his history.

"I was in the boats at six years old," he said; "for there was always something I could do. During the night-fishing, unless I went with father, I was alone; and I had hours of such awful terrors that I am sad only to remember them; it was better to freeze out on the sea, if father would let me go with him. I was often hungry and often weary; I had toothaches and earaches that I never spoke of; I was frequently so sleepy that I fell down in the boat. And I had no mother to kiss me or pity me, and the neighbors were shy and far off. Father was not cross or unkind; he just did not understand. Even in those days I wondered why God made little lads to be so miserable and to suffer so much."

He spoke then in a very guarded way about that revelation in the boat, for he felt rebuked for his want of faith in it; and he said sorrowfully, as he left the subject, "Why, then, should God send angels to men? They are feared of them while they are present, and they doubt them when they are gone away. He sent one to comfort me, and I denied it to my own heart; yes, even though I sorely needed the comfort."

Then he took John to Shetland with him. He showed him, in strong, simple words, the old Norse town, with its gray skies and its gray seas, and its fishing-smacks hanging to the rushing sides of foaming mountains. He described the hoary cliffs and their world of sea-birds, the glorious auroras, the heavenly summers, and the deadly chillness of the winter fogs as one drift after another passed in dim and desolate majesty over the sea and land.

Slowly and with some hesitation he got to Nanna in her little stone hut, braiding her straw and nursing her crippled baby. The tears came into his eyes, he clasped his knees with his hands as if to steady himself, while he spoke rapidly of her marriage with Nicol Sinclair, the drowning of her father and brothers, the cruelty of her husband, his desertion, his return, Nanna's terror of losing Vala, the fatal typhus, her desolation, and her spiritual anguish about Vala's condition. All these things he told John with that powerful eloquence which is born of living, intense feeling.

John was greatly moved by the whole simple, tragic story, but he spoke only on the last topic, for it seemed to him to dwarf all other sorrow. It roused his indignation, and he said it was a just and holy anger. He wondered how men, and especially mothers, could worship a God who was supposed to damn little children before they were born. He vowed that neither Moloch nor Baal, nor any pagan deity, had been so brutal. He was amazed that ministers believing such a doctrine dared to marry. What special right had they to believe their children would all be elect? And if there was a shadow of doubt on this subject, how awful was their responsibility! Nanna's scruples, he said, were the only possible outcome of a conscientious, unselfish soul believing the devilish doctrine. And he cried out with enthusiasm:

"Nanna is to be honored! Oh, for a conscience as tender and void of offense toward God! I will go to Shetland and kiss the hem of her garment! She is a woman in ten thousand!"

"Well, then," said David, softly, "I shall take comfort to her."

"To think," said John, who was still moved by a holy anger, "to think that God should have created this beautiful world as a nursery for hell! that he should have made such a woman as Nanna to suckle devils! No, no, David!" he said, suddenly calming himself; "thee could never believe such things of thy God."

"I was taught them early and late. I can say the Confession of Faith backward, I am sure."

"Let no man-made creed impose itself on thee, David—enter into thee, and possess thee, and take the place of thy soul. The voice that spoke from Sinai and from Bethlehem is still speaking. And man's own soul is an oracle, if he will only listen to it—the inward, instant sense of a present God, and of his honorable, true, and only Son Christ Jesus."

"I will listen, if God will speak."

"Never thee mind catechisms and creeds and confessions. The Word of God was before them, and the Word will be the Word when catechisms and confessions are cast into the dusty museums of ancient things, with all the other shackles of the world in bondage. David, there is in every good man a spiritual center, answering to a higher spiritual center in the universe. All controversies come back to this."

"I wish, John Priestly, that you could see Nanna, and speak comfort to her heart."

"That must be thy message, David. And be sure that thee knows well the children's portion in the Scriptures. Thee must show Nanna that *theirs is the kingdom*. What we win through great tribulation they inherit through the love of the Father. *Theirs is the kingdom*; and there is no distinction of elect or non-elect, as I read the title."

"I count the hours now until I am able to travel. I long for the sea that stretches nor'ard to the ice, and the summer days, when the sunset brightens the midnight. No need to egg me on. I am all the time thinking of the old town growing out of the mist, and I know how I shall feel when I stand on the pier again among the fishers, when I hurry through the clean, quiet streets, while the kind people nod and smile, and call to each other, 'Here is David Borson come back again.'"

"And Nanna?"

"She is the heart of my longing."

"And thee is taking her glad tidings of great joy."

"I am that. So there is great hurry in my heart, for I like not to sit in the sunshine and know that Nanna is weeping in the dark."

"Thee must not be discouraged if she be at first unable to believe thy report."

"The hour will come. Nanna was ever a seeker after God. She will listen joyfully. She will take the cup of salvation, and drink it with thanksgiving. We shall stand together in the light, loving God and fearing God, but not afraid of him. Faith in Christ will set her free."

"But lean hard upon God's Word, David. There is light enough and help enough for every strait of life in it. Let thy creed lie at rest. There are many doors to scientific divinity, but there is only one door to heaven. And I will tell thee this thing, David: if men had to be good theologians before they were good Christians, the blessed heaven would be empty."

"Yet, John, my theology was part of my very life. Nothing to me was once more certain than that men and women were in God's hand as clay in the potter's. And as some vessels are made to honor, and some to dishonor, so some men were made for salvation and honor, and others for rejection and dishonor."

"Clay in the potter's hand! And some for honor, and some for dishonor! We will even grant that much; but tell me, David, does the potter ever make his vessels for *the express purpose of breaking them*? No, no, David! He is not willing that *any* should perish. Christ is not going to lose what he has bought with his blood. The righteous are planted as trees by the watercourses, but God does not plant any tree for fuel."

"He is a good God, and his name is Love."

"So, then, thee is going back to Shetland with glad tidings for many a soul. What will thy hands find to do for thy daily bread?"

"I shall go back to the boats and the nets and lines."

"Would thee like to have a less dangerous way of earning thy bread? My father has a great business in the city, and thee could drive one of the big drays that go to the docks."

"I could not. I can carry a ship through any sea a ship can live in; I could not drive a Shetland shelty down an empty street. I am only a simple sea-dog. I love the sea. Men say for sure it is in my heart and my blood. I must live on the sea. When my hour comes to die, I hope the sea will keep my body in one of her clean, cool graves. If God gives me Nanna, and we have sons and daughters, they shall have a happy childhood and a good schooling. Then I will put all the boys in the boats, and the girls shall learn to grow like their mother, and, if it please God, they shall marry good men and good fishers."

"It seems to me that the life of a fisher is a very hard one, and withal that it hath but small returns."

"Fishers have their good and their bad seasons. They take their food direct from the hand of God; so, then, good or bad, it is all right. Fishers have their loves and joys and sorrows; birth and marriage and death come to them as to others. They have the same share of God's love, the same Bible, the same hope of eternal life, that the richest men and women have. It is enough."

"And hard lives have their compensations, David. Doubtless the fisherman's life has its peculiar blessings?"

"It has. The fisher's life is as free from temptation as a life can be. He *has* to trust God a great deal; if he did not he would very seldom go into the boats at all."

"Yet he holds the ocean 'in the hollow of his hand.'"

"That is true. I never feel so surely held in the hollow of his hand as when the waves are as high as my masthead, and my boat smashes into the black pit below. There is none but God then. Thank you, Friend John, but I shall live and die a fisherman."

"Would thee care to change Shetland for some warmer and less stormy climate?"

"Would a man care to change his own father and mother for any other father and mother? Stern and hard was my poor father, and he knew not how to love; but his memory is dear to me, and I would not break the tie between us—no, not to be the son of a king! My native land is a poor land, but I have thought of her green and purple moors among gardens full of roses. Shetland is my *home*, and home is sweet and fair and dear."

"Traveling Zionward, David, we have often to walk in the wilderness. Thee hast dwelt in Skye and in Shetland; what other lands hast thee seen?"

"I have been east as far as Smyrna. I sat there and read the message of 'the First and the Last' to its church. And I went to Athens, and stood where St. Paul had once stood. And I have seen Rome and Naples and Genoa and Marseilles, and many of the Spanish and French ports. I have pulled oranges from the trees, and great purple grapes from the vines, and even while I was eating them longed for the oat-cakes and fresh fish of Shetland."

"Rome and Naples and Athens! Then, David, thee hast seen the fairest cities on the earth."

"And yet, Friend John, what hells I saw in them! I was taken through great buildings where men and women die of dreadful pain. I saw other buildings where men and women could eat and sleep, and could not think or love or know. I saw drinking-hells and gambling-hells. I saw men in dark and awful prisons, men living in poverty and filth and blasphemy, without hope for this world or the next. I saw men die on the scaffold. And, John, I have often wondered if this world were hell. Are we put here in low, or lower, or lowest hell to work out our salvation, and so at last, through great tribulation, win our weary way back to heaven?"

John Priestly was silent a few moments ere he answered: "If that were even so, there is still comfort, David. For if we make our bed in any of such hells,—mind, *we* make it,—even there we are not beyond the love and the pity of the Infinite One. For when the sorrows of hell compassed David of old, he cried unto God, and he delivered him from his strong enemy, and brought him forth into a large place. So, then, David, though good men may get into hell, they do not need to stay there."

"I know that by experience, John. Have I not been in the lowest pit, in darkness, in the deeps, in that lowest hell of the soul where I had no God to pray to? For how could I pray to a God so cruel that I did not dare to become a father, lest he should elect my children to damnation? a God so unjust that he loved without foresight of faith or good works, and hated because it was his pleasure to hate, and to ordain the hated to dishonor and wrath?"[4]

"And yet, David?"

"In my distress my soul cried out, '*God pity me! God pity me!* And even while I so wronged him he sent from above—he sent you, John; he took me, he drew me out of many waters,—for great was his mercy toward me,—and he delivered my soul from the lowest hell."

---

[4]

Confession of Faith, chap. 3, secs. v-vii; chap. 16, sec. vii.

<hr size=2 width="100%" align=center>

XII
"AT LAST IT IS PEACE"

A week after this conversation David was near Lerwick. It was very early in the morning, and the sky was gray and the sea was gray, and through the vapory veiling the little town looked gray and silent as a city in a dream. During the voyage he had thought of himself always as hastening at once to Nanna's house, but as soon as his feet touched the quay he hesitated. The town appeared to be asleep; there was only here and there a thin column of peat smoke from the chimneys, and the few people going about their simple business in the misty morning were not known to him. Probably, also, he had some unreasonable expectation, for he looked sadly around, and, sighing, said:

"To be sure, such a thing would never happen, except in a dream."

After all, it seemed best that he should go first to Barbara Traill's. She would give him a cup of tea, and while he drank it he could send one of Glumm's little lads with a message to Nanna. There was nothing of cowardice in this determination; it was rather that access of reverential love which, as it draws nearer, puts its own desire and will at the feet of the beloved one.

Barbara's door stood open, and she was putting fresh fuel under the hanging tea-kettle. The smell of the peat smoke was homely and pleasant to David; he sniffed it eagerly as he called out:

"Well, then, mother, good morning!"

She raised herself quickly, and turned her broad, kind face to him. A strange shadow crossed it when she saw David, but she answered affectionately:

"Well, then, David, here we meet again!"

Then she hastened the morning meal, and as she did so asked question after question about his welfare and adventures, until David said a little impatiently:

"There is enough of this talk, mother. Speak to me now of Nanna Sinclair. Is she well?"

"Your aunt Sabiston is dead. There was a great funeral, I can tell you that. She has left all her money to the kirk and the societies; and a white stone as high as two men has come from Aberdeen for her grave. Well, so it is. And you must know, also, that my son has married himself, and not to my liking, and so he has gone from me; and your room is empty and ready, if you wish it so; and–"

"Yes, yes, Barbara! Keep your room for me, and I will pay the price of it."

"I will do that gladly; and as for the price, we shall have no words about that."

"All this is well enough, but, mother! mother! what is there to hide from me? Speak with a straight tongue. Where is Nanna?"

Then Barbara said plainly, "Nanna is dead."

With a cry of amazed anguish David leaped to his feet, instinctively covering his ears with his hands, for he could not bear such words to enter them. *"Dead!"* he whispered; and Barbara saw him reeling and swaying like a tottering pillar. She pushed a chair toward him, and was thankful that he had strength left to take its support. But she made no outcry, and called in none of the neighbors. Quietly she stood a little way off, while David, in a death-like silence, fought away the swooning, drowning wave which was making his heart stand still and his limbs fail him. For she knew the nature of the suffering man–knew that when he came to himself there would be none but God could intermeddle in his heart's bitterness and loss.

After a sharp struggle David opened his eyes, and Barbara gave him a drink of cold water; but she offered neither advice nor consolation. Only when David said, "I am sick, mother, and I will go to my room and lie down on my bed," she answered:

"My dear lad, that is the right way. Sleep, if sleep you can."

About sunsetting David asked Barbara for food; and as she prepared it he sat by the open window, silent and stupefied, dominated by the somber inertia of hopeless sorrow. When he began to eat, Barbara took from a china jar two papers, and gave them to him.

"I promised Nanna to put them into your hands," she said.

ON THE WAY TO NANNA'S COTTAGE.

"When did she die?"

"Last December, the fourteenth day."

"Did you see her on that day?"

"I was there early in the morning, for I saw there was snow to fall. She was dead at the noon hour."

"You saw her go away?"

"No; I was afraid of the storm. I left her at ten o'clock. She could not then speak, but she gave me the papers. We had talked of them before."

"Then did she die alone?"

"She did not. I went into the next cottage and told Christine Yell that it was the last hour with Nanna; and she said, 'I will go to her,' and so she did."

"You should have stayed, mother."

"My lad, the snow was already falling, and I had to hasten across the moor, as there was very good reason to do."

Then David went out, and Barbara watched him take the road that led to Nanna's empty cottage. The door opened readily to the lifted latch, and he entered the forsaken room. The peat fire had long ago burned itself to ashes. The rose-plant, which had been Nanna's delight, had withered away on its little shelf by the window. But the neighbors had swept the floor and put the simple furniture in order. David drew the bolt across the door, and opened the papers which Nanna had left for him. The first was a bequest to him of the cottage and all within it; the second was but a little slip on which the dying woman had written her last sad messages to him:

Oh, my love! my love! Farewell forever! I am come to the end of my life. I am going away, and I know not where to. All is dark. But I have cast myself at His feet, and said, "Thy will be done!"

<hr size=2 width="40%" align=center>

I am still alive, David. I have been alone all night, and every breath has been a death-pang. How can His eternal purpose need my bitter suffering? Oh, that God would pity me! His will be done!

<hr size=2 width="40%" align=center>

My love, it is nearly over. *I have seen Vala!* At last it is peace–peace! His will be done! Mercy–mercy–mercy–

These pitiful despairs and farewells were written in a large, childish hand, and on a poor sheet of paper. David spread this paper upon Vala's couch, and, kneeling down, covered it with tears and kisses; but anon he lifted it up toward heaven, and prayed as men pray when they feel prayer to be an immediate and veritable thing–when they detain God, and clasp his feet, and cling to his robe, and will not let him go until he bless them.

Christine Yell had seen David enter the cottage, and after an hour had passed she went to the door intending to speak to him; but she heard the solemn, mysterious voice of the man praying, and she went away and called her neighbors, Margaret Jarl and Elga Fae and Thora Thorson. And they talked of David a little, and then Magnus Thorson, the father-in-law of Thora, being a very old man, went alone into Nanna's cottage to see David. And after a while the women were called, and Christine took with her a plate of fish and bread which she had prepared; and David was glad of their sympathy.

They sat down outside the door. The tender touch of the gray gloaming softened the bleak cliffs and the brown moorland, and the heavens were filled with stars. Then softly and solemnly Christine spoke of Nanna's long, hard fight with death, and of the spiritual despair which had intensified her suffering.

"It was in season and out of season that she was at Vala's grave," said Christine, "and kneeling and lying on the cold ground above her; and the end was–what could only be looked for–a cough and a fever, and the slow consumption that wasted her away."

"Was there none of you to comfort her?"

"It is true, David, that the child was never baptized," said Christine; "so, then, what comfort could there be for her? And then she began to think that God had never loved her."

"Thanks to the Best, she knows now how far wrong she was," said David, fervently; "she knows now that his love is from everlasting to everlasting. Her poor heart, wearied with so many sorrows and troubled by so many fears, has tasted one supreme happiness–that God is love."

"She thought for sure that he was continually angry with her. 'If he had cared for my soul,' she said to me, one day, 'he would not have let me marry Nicol Sinclair. He would have kept his hand about me until my cousin David Borson came from the Hebrides. And if he had cared for my poor bairn he would not, by this and that, have prevented the minister coming to baptize her."

"Was she long ill?" asked David.

"At the beginning of last winter she became too ill to go to the ordinances, and too feared to open her Bible, lest she should read her own condemnation in it; and so gradually she seemed to lose all hope, either for this life or the next one. And folk wearied of her complaining, I think."

"The elders and the minister, did they not try to comfort her?"

"At first Elder Peterson and Elder Hoag came to see her; but Nanna put strange questions to them–questions they could not answer; and they said the minister could not answer them, either–no, nor the whole assembly of the kirk of Scotland. And I was hearing that the minister was angered by her words and her doubting, and he told her plainly 'women had no call to speer after the "why" of God's purposes.' And indeed, David, she was very outspoken,–for she was fretful with pain and fever,–and she told him that she was not thankful to go to hell for the glory and honor of God, and that, moreover, she did not want to go to heaven if Vala was not there. And when the minister said, '*Whist*, woman!'–for he was frightened at her words,–she would not be still, but went on to wonder how fathers and mothers could be happy, even in the very presence of God, if their sons and daughters were wandering in the awful outer darkness; and, moreover, she said she was not grateful to God for life, and she thought her consent to coming into life on such hard terms ought to have been first asked."

And Christine looked at David, and ceased speaking, for she was afraid that her words would both anger and trouble the young man. But David's eyes were full of happy tears, and there was a tender smile round his mouth. He was thinking of the glad surprises that Nanna must have had–she who belonged to the God of compassions. After all her shuddering questions and lamentable doubts and cruel pain, the everlasting arms under her; Vala and her beloved dead to comfort her; ineffable peace; unclouded joy; the night past; the last tear wiped away! At that moment he felt that it was too late to weep for Nanna; indeed, he smiled like one full of blessed thought. And Christine, a little irritated by the unexpected mood, did not further try to smooth over the hard facts of the lonely woman's death-bed.

"The minister was angry with her, and he said God was angry. And Nanna said, well, then, she knew that he did not care about her perishing; it was all one to him. A little happiness would have saved her, and he refused her the smallest joy; and she did not see how crushing the poor and broken-hearted in the dust increased his glory. The minister told her she was resisting God, and she said, no; that was not possible. God was her master, and he smote her, and perhaps had the right to do so; but she was not his child: no father would treat a child so hardly as he had treated her. She was a slave, and must submit, and weep and die at the corner of the highway. And, to be sure, the minister did not think of her pain and her woman's heart,—what men do?—and he thought it right to speak hard words to her. And then Nanna said she wished they would all leave her alone with her sorrow, and so they did."

Then, suddenly and swiftly as a flash of light, a word came to David. His heart burned, and his tongue was loosened, and then and there he preached to the old man and the three women the unsearchable riches of the cross of Christ. He glorified God because Nanna had learned Christ at the radiant feet of Christ, in the joy and love of the redeemed. He took his Bible from his pocket, and repeated all the blessed words he had marked and learned. Until the midnight moon climbed cold and bright to the zenith he spoke. And old Magnus Thorson stood up, leaning on his staff, full of holy wonder, and the women softly sobbed and prayed at his feet. And when they parted there was in every heart a confident acceptance of David's closing words:

"Whoever rests, however feebly, on the eternal mercy shall live forever."

After this "call" sleep was impossible to David. That insight which changes faith into knowledge had comforted him concerning his dead. He lay down on Vala's couch, and he felt sure that Nanna's smile filled the silence like a spell; for there are still moments when we have the transcendental faculties of the illuminated who, as the apostle says, "have tasted of the powers of the world to come"—still moments when we feel that Jacob's ladder yet stands between heaven and earth, and that we can see the angels ascending and descending upon it. He was so still that he could hear the beating of his own heart, but clear and vivid as light his duty spread out before him. He had found his vocation, and, oh, how rapidly men grow under the rays of that invisible sun!

The next morning he went to see the minister. He was seated, writing his sermon, precisely as David had found him on the occasion of his last visit. So much had happened to David since that morning that he found it difficult to believe nothing had happened to the minister. He looked up at the interruption with the same slight annoyance, but the moment he saw David his manner changed. He rose up quickly and went to meet him, and as he clasped his hand looked with curious intentness into his face.

"You are much changed, David," he said. "What has happened to you?"

"Everything, nearly, minister. The David Borson who left here two years ago is dead and buried. I have been born again."

"That is a great experience. Sit down and tell me about it."

"Yes, minister, but first I must speak of Nanna Sinclair."

"She is dead, David; that is true."

"She has gone home. She has gone to the God who loved her."

"I–hope so."

"I know it is so. Nanna loved God, and those who love God in life will find no difficulty in going to him after life is over."

"She had a hard life, and it was all in the dark to her."

"But at the death-hour it was light, though the light was not of this world." And David told the minister about the farewell message she had written him, and its final happy words, "*At last it is peace–peace!*" He could not bear that any eyes should see the paper, or any hand touch it, but his own; but he wished all to know that at the death-hour God had comforted her.

"She suffered a great deal, David."

"What ailed her, minister?"

"What ails the lamp, David, when it goes out? There is no oil, that is all. Nanna used up all her strength in weeping and feeling; the oil of life wastes quickly in that way."

"O minister, I am so sorry that I left her! It was selfish and cruel. I wish now that I could cover her hands with kisses, and ask her pardon on my knees; but I find nothing but a grave."

"Ah, David, it is death that forces us to see the selfishness that comes into our best affections. Self permitted you to give all you had to Nanna, but forbade you to give yourself. There was self even in your self-surrender to God. If you could have seen that long, long disappointed look in Nanna's eyes, and the pale lips that asked so little from you–"

"O minister, spare me! She asked only, 'Stay near me, David'; and I might have stayed and comforted her to the end. Oh, for one hour—one hour only! But neither to-day nor to-morrow, nor through all eternity, shall I have the opportunity to love and soothe which I threw away because it hurt me and made my heart ache." And David bowed his head in his hands and wept bitterly.

Alas! love, irreparably wronged, possesses these eternal memories; and the soul, forced to weep for opportunities gone forever, has these inconsolable refinements of tenderness. "One hour—one hour only!" was the cry of David's soul. And the answer was, "No, never! She has carried away her sorrow. You may, indeed, meet her where all tears are dried and forgotten; but while she did weep you were not there; you had left her alone, and your hour to comfort her has gone forever."

After a short silence the minister went to his desk, and brought from it David's purse, and he laid it, with the will that had been written, before him. "It is useless now," he said. "Nanna has need of nothing you can give her."

"Did it do any good, minister?"

"Yes, a great deal. When Nanna was no longer able to come to the kirk, I went to see her. She was miserably sick and poor, and it made my heart ache to watch her thin, trembling fingers trying to knit. I took her work gently out of her hands, and said, 'You are not able to hold the needles, Nanna, and you have no need to try to do so. There is provision made for all your wants.' And she flared up like whin-bushes set on fire, and said she had asked neither kirk nor town for help, and that she trusted in God to deliver her from this life before she had to starve or take a beggar's portion."

"O minister, if God had not comforted me concerning her, you would break my heart. What did you say to the dear woman?"

"I said, 'It is neither kirk nor town nor almsgivers that have provided for your necessity, Nanna; it is your cousin David Borson.' And when she heard your name she began to cry, '*O David! David!*' And after I had let her weep awhile I said, 'You will let your cousin do for you at this hour, Nanna?' And she answered, 'Oh, yes; I will take any favor from David. It was like him to think of me. Oh, that he would come back!' So I sent her every week ten shillings until she died, and then I saw that she was decently laid beside her mother and her little child; and I paid all expenses from the money you left. There is a reckoning of them in the papers. Count it, with the money."

"I will not count after you, minister."

"Well, David, God has counted between us. It is all right to the last bawbee. Now tell where you have been, and what you have seen and suffered; for it is written on your face that you have seen many hard days."

Then David told all about his wanderings and his shipwreck, and the mercy of God to him through his servant John Priestly. But when he tried to speak of the new revelation of the gospel that had come to him, he found his lips closed. The fire that had burned on them the night before, when he spoke under the midnight sky to the old fisherman and the fisherwives, was dead and cold, and he could not kindle it; so he said to himself, "It is not yet the hour." And he went out of the manse without telling one of all the glorious things he had resolved to tell. Neither was he troubled by the omission. He could wait God's time. God, who has made the heart, can always touch the heart, but he felt that just then his words would irritate rather than move; besides, it was not necessary for him to speak unless he got the message. He could not constrain another soul, but there was One who led by invisible cords.

As they stood a moment at the manse door the minister said, "Your aunt Sabiston has gone the way of all flesh."

"I heard tell," answered David. "How did she go?"

"Like herself–grim and steadfast to the last. She would not take to her bed; she met death in her chair. When the doctor told her Death was in the room, she stood up, and welcomed him to her house, and said, 'I have long been waiting for your release.' I tried to talk to her, but she told me to my face that I had nothing to do with her soul. 'If I am lost, I am lost,' she said; 'and if I am chosen, who shall lay anything to the charge of God's elect?' She said she believed herself to be the child of God, and that, though she had made some sore stumbles and been fractious and ill to guide, she had done no worse than many of his well-loved bairns, and she expected no worse welcome home. 'I have been long away, minister,' she sighed, 'getting on to a century away, and I'll be glad to win home again.' And those were her last words."

"God be merciful to her! In this world, I think, she was an unjust and cruel woman."

"She was so, then, without moral disquietude. The sin had got into her soul, and she was comfortable with it. God is her judge. He only knew her aright. She left her money wisely and for good ends."

"I heard tell, to the kirk and the societies and the freedom fund. Yet she had kinsfolk in the Orkneys."

"They are all very rich. They went to lawyers about her property, but Mistress Sabiston had made all too fast and sure for any one to alter. She was a woman that would have her way, dead or alive."

"Well, then, this time, it seems, her way is a good way."

After this David settled his life very much on the old lines. He went to live in Nanna's cottage, and returned to the boats and the fishing with Groat's sons. As for his higher duty, that vocation that had come to him on that blessed night when God opened his mouth and he spoke wonderful and gracious things of his law, he was never for a moment recreant to it. But the kingdom of God frequently comes without observation. To preach a sermon, that was a thing far outside David's possibilities. The power of the church, and its close and exclusive privileges, were at that day in Shetland papal in prerogative. David never dreamed of encroaching on them; nor, indeed, would public opinion have permitted him to do so.

As it was, there grew gradually a feeling of unrest about David. Though he was humble and devout in all kirk exercises, it was known that the people gathered round him not only in his own cottage, but at Groat's and Barbara Traill's, and that he spoke to them of the everlasting gospel as never man had spoken before to them. It was known that when the boats lay stilly rocking on the water, waiting for the "take," David, sitting among his mates, reasoned with them on the love of God, until every face of clay flushed with a radiance quite different from mere color–a radiance that was a direct spiritual emanation, a shining of the soul through mere matter. And as these men were all theologians in a measure, with their "creed" and "evidences" at their tongues' end, it was a wonderful joy to watch their doubts, like the needle verging to the pole, tremble and tremble into certainty.

"WENT IN AND OUT AMONG HIS MATES."

In about three years such opposition as David roused was strong enough to induce the kirk to consider his behavior. The minister sent for him, and in the privacy of his study David's opportunity came at last. For he spoke so eloquently and mightily of the mercy of the Infinite One that the minister covered his face, and when the young man ceased speaking, he looked tenderly at him, and sent him away with his blessing. And afterward he said to the elders:

"There is nothing to call a session anent. David Borson has been to the school of Christ, and he is learned in the Scriptures. We will not silence him, lest haply we be found to be fighting against God."

Thus for many a year David went in and out among his mates and friends, living the gospel in their sight. The memory of Nanna filled his heart; he loved no other woman, but every desolate and sorrowful woman found in him a friend and a helper. And he drew the little children like a magnet. He was the elder brother of every boy and girl who claimed his love; his hands were ever ready to help them, his heart was ever ready to love them. And in such blessed service he grew nobly aged.

He had come to Shetland when the islands were very far off, when the Norse element ruled them, and the Christianized men and women of the sagas dwelt alone in the strong, quaint stone houses they had built. He lived to see the influx of the southern race and influences, the coming of modern travel and civilization; but he never altered his life, for in its simple, pious dignity it befitted any era.

Now, it is noticeable that good men very often have their desire about the manner of their death. And God so favored his servant David Borson. He went out alone one day in his boat, and a sudden storm came up from the northeast. He did not return. Some said there had been no time to take in the boat's sail, and that she must have gone down with her canvas blowing; others thought she had become unmanageable and drifted into some of the dangerous "races" near the coast.

But, this manner or that manner, David went to heaven as he desired, "by the way of the sea," and God found his body a resting-place among its cool, clean graves—a sepulcher that no man knoweth of, nor shall know until the mighty angel sets his right foot upon the sea, and swears that there shall "be time no longer."

Milton Keynes UK
Ingram Content Group UK Ltd.
UKHW030625061024
449204UK00004B/316